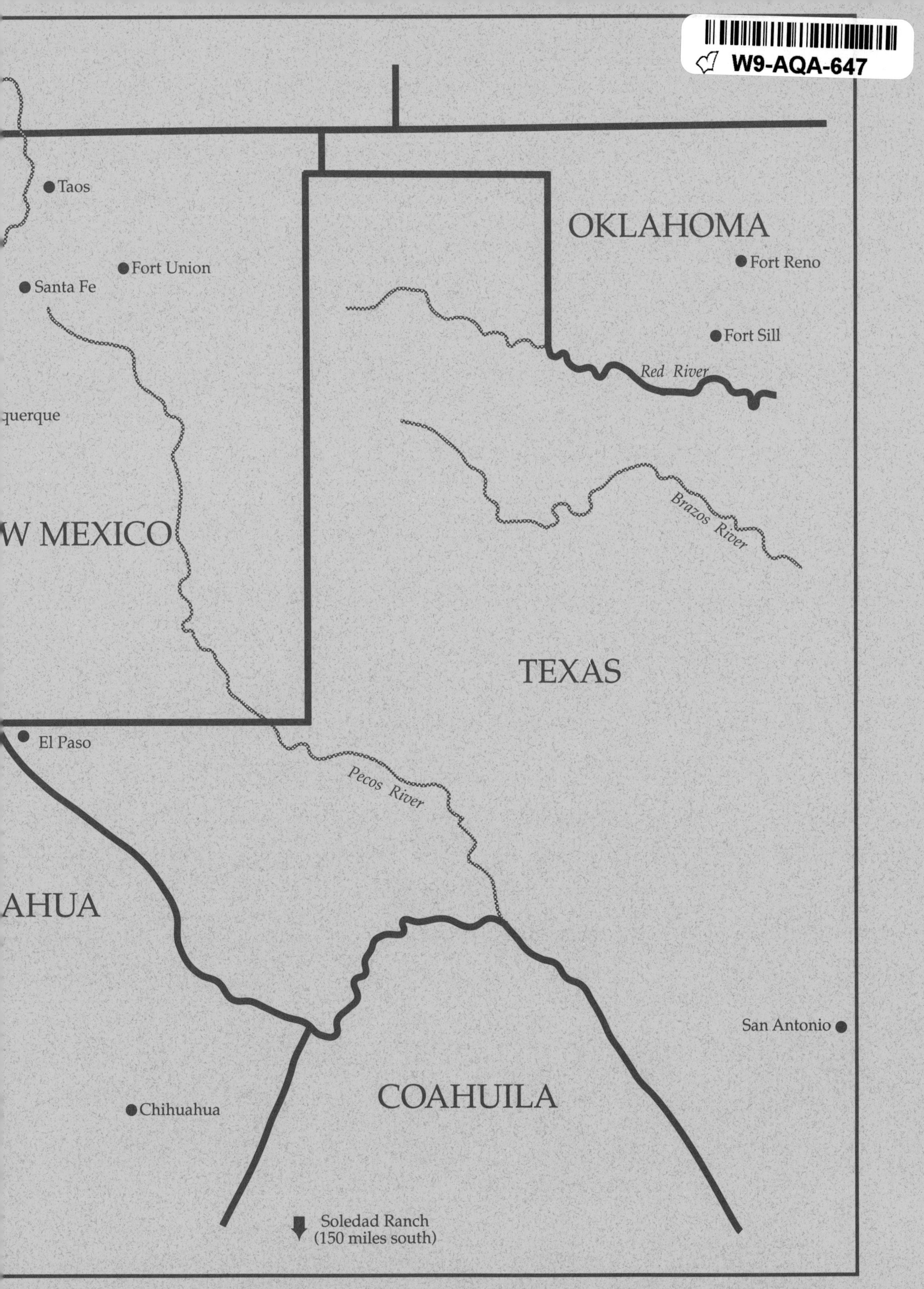
W9-AQA-647
Taos
OKLAHOMA
Fort Reno
Fort Union
Santa Fe
Fort Sill
Red River
querque
Brazos River
W MEXICO
TEXAS
El Paso
Pecos River
AHUA
San Antonio
COAHUILA
Chihuahua
Soledad Ranch
(150 miles south)

Frederic Remington's Southwest

FREDERIC REMINGTON

Frederic Remington's Southwest

JAMES K. BALLINGER

PHOENIX ART MUSEUM
PHOENIX, ARIZONA

This catalogue has been published in conjunction with the exhibition
Frederic Remington's Southwest

PHOENIX ART MUSEUM
January 4 through March 15, 1992

MEMPHIS BROOKS MUSEUM OF ART
April 19 through June 21, 1992

JOSLYN ART MUSEUM
July 11 through September 6, 1992

The exhibition has been organized by the Phoenix Art Museum.
This project is made possible by a grant from Phelps Dodge Corporation.
Additional funding is from the Western Art Associates
of the Phoenix Art Museum,
First Interstate Bank of Arizona
and Salt River Project, Phoenix.

Library of Congress Cataloging-in-Publication Data

Ballinger, James K.
Frederic Remington's Southwest / James K. Ballinger.
p. cm.
Catalog of an exhibition held at the Phoenix Art Museum. Jan. 4–Mar. 15, 1992, Memphis Brooks Museum of Art, Apr. 19–June 21, 1992, and Joslyn Art Museum, July 11–Sept. 13, 1992.
Includes bibliographical references.
ISBN 0-910407-25-8
1. Remington, Frederic, 1861–1909 — Exhibitions. 2. Southwest, New, in art — Exhibitions. 3. Indians of North America — Pictorial works — Exhibitions. I. Phoenix Art Museum. II. Memphis Brooks Museum of Art. III. Joslyn Art Museum. IV. Title.
N6537.R4A4 1992
709' .2 — dc20

Front cover: The Cowboy, 1902, oil on canvas. Amon Carter Museum, Fort Worth, Texas
Frontispiece: Cavalryman of the Line, Mexico, 1889, oil on canvas. Amon Carter Museum, Fort Worth, Texas

Acknowledgments

COORDINATING SPECIAL EXHIBITIONS for museum visitors is perhaps the most gratifying aspect of museum work. Thousands of individuals, young and old, are introduced, or re-introduced to fascinating aspects of myriad cultures which exist, or have existed on our planet. These projects and the accompanying publications and programs are the result of scores of individuals' help and teamwork. "Frederic Remington's Southwest" is no different.

This project is related to a previous undertaking, the opportunity to contribute a volume on Remington to the Library of American Art series published by Harry N. Abrams, Inc. in association with the National Museum of American Art. During research and preparation of that volume, published in 1989, this exhibition was conceived. Thus, I would like to again acknowledge my gratitude to everyone involved with that book.

No exhibition such as "Frederic Remington's Southwest" is possible without the encouragement and enthusiasm of those individuals and institutions which make their works of art available to a wider viewing audience. To each of them, who are listed individually with their loans elsewhere in this volume, I extend my thanks.

Over the years I have drawn assistance from those who were closer to Remington than I. Peter Hassrick, Director of the Buffalo Bill Historical Center, has always shared his insights learned during the past two decades, and Melissa Webster of his staff has provided many details from their computerized raisonné. The staff at the Frederic Remington Art Museum, under the leadership of Lowell McAllister, has likewise, always been ready to respond. Mark VanBenschoten and Laura Foster have been cordial and insightful to this study. Because of Remington's long-time popularity, his works have regularly changed hands among collectors. Several works in this exhibition were sought out with the help of Rudy Wunderlich and Gerald Peters whose galleries have long been involved with great western American art.

Closer to home, many individuals affiliated with our museum have been extremely helpful and supportive while bringing this project to fruition. Barbara Gutierrez, Denise Stefanisin, Slawa Ciula, Clayton Kirking and Linda Marrie gathered information helpful in the selection of works and development of the catalogue essay. Melissa Keen and Mary Vargas handled many of the clerical tasks. Mark Sanders designed the publication. Heather Northway coordinated all of the loans and shipping arrangements. David Restad, Gene Koeneman and Bob Gates creatively designed the installation of the exhibition. And, Jan Krulick provided a wide variety of interpretive programs for the public.

All of the above activity would not have taken place without strong financial commitments. Phelps Dodge Corporation, founded in Arizona about the time of Remington's first visits, has provided major funding for this project. Additional support has come from the Western Art Associates of the Phoenix Art Museum, and First Interstate Bank of Arizona, one of the state's oldest financial institutions, and Salt River Project, founded during Theodore Roosevelt's presidency.

The desire of the staffs at the Memphis Brooks Museum of Art and the Joslyn Art Museum to take "Frederic Remington's Southwest" to other geographic locations is also exciting. Such activity helps achieve the goals of all exhibitions.

James K. Ballinger
Director

Preface

FREDERIC REMINGTON'S CAPITALIZATION on the images of the Southwest catapulted him to stardom in the eyes of the late 19th century American public. Few young artists experienced such a meteoric rise to popularity. Between January 1886, when his first Geronimo images were reproduced, and the end of 1888, over two hundred works by Remington were published in national magazines. Many articles were also written by the artist for which he provided his own visual imagery. During this time period he began his career as a fine artist by entering southwestern works in two prestigious national exhibitions, the American Watercolor Society annual exhibition and the semi-annual display at the National Academy of Design in New York City. He was quickly invited to become an associate member of the National Academy. This ambitious young artist was brimming with confidence by 1889 when he created two large paintings which drew national and international attention.

Remington's early death in 1909, at the age of forty-eight, ended the career of a man who had become one of America's best known and most financially successful artists. His intense, frequent experiences in the Southwest prior to 1900 served as a reservoir of subject matter throughout his career enabling him to become an illustrator, a painter, a journalist, a novelist and a sculptor. The development of his career as it pertains to the Southwest is the subject of this publication and the exhibition it accompanies. To list Remington's "career firsts" as they relate to "his Southwest" serves as an outline of this project — first illustration, first entry in the National Academy of Design, first commissioned painting, first sculpture,

Frederic Remington at about age 25, *n.d., ink drawing by Theodore Davis. Courtesy of Mongerson Wunderlich Gallery, Chicago, Illinois*

first color print, first painting acquired for a museum, and his only monumental sculpture.

Frederic Remington's Southwest developed very clearly in his mind, and was a geographic region much different than we think of today. Arizona and New Mexico were territories when Remington first arrived in 1885. His initial visit to Indian Territory was during the previous year when he briefly owned a sheep ranch in south central Kansas, just a short ride from the various Reservations carved out of what is today Oklahoma. Investing much of his inheritance following his father's 1880 death, the twenty-two-year-old joined a Yale classmate in the ranching business in Kansas, imagining a rather gentlemanly venture. Remington had planned to take casual sketching trips south into Indian Territory, but hard work and constant attention to the animals, land and buildings prevented this. Years later, this region around Fort Sill and Fort Reno (pages 3 and 4) would serve as a beginning point for trips or a concluding destination for Remington's southwest travels. As Remington made sojourns for visual material, his experiences created the geography of "his Southwest" because public attention focused on the Indian Wars of the West and Southwest following the Civil War. The Apaches, under Geronimo's leadership, freely roamed between southwestern New Mexico, southeastern Arizona and northern Mexico, thus Remington's images are not specific to a location. In addition, his ultimate interest in the Mexican military took him to Mexico City as well as the northern states of Coahuila, Chihuahua and Sonora. Over a two decade period the artist traveled throughout these

Agency Near Sill (In the Betting Ring — Comanches), *1889, oil on canvas (black and white). Collection IBM Corporation, Armonk, New York*

unique areas, visiting military installations, Indian Agencies and ranches on eleven separate occasions.

As a youth Remington was a rough and ready type, who had difficulty concentrating on his studies. He had a great curiosity about life in the West, and was strong-willed about building a career around southwestern American ranch life and military events. Born in upstate New York, Remington had limited formal art training. His parents, Seth Pierre and Clara Sackrider Remington were of solid upper middle-class families in Canton, New York, and wanted the best for their only child, sending him to a private military academy and then to Yale. Remington's father was a local Civil War hero, who owned the newspaper in Canton and was very active in Republican politics. Remington's educational path reflects a boy who was being prepared to follow in his father's footsteps. He did not object because he idolized his father. Cornell University had been his first choice as a college where he intended to study journalism. Instead, he enrolled at Yale in September, 1878, matriculating in their recently formed School of Art which followed a very academic European derived curriculum. Whatever Remington's dreams were at that time they were destroyed in February 1880 when his father died, forcing the young man to leave

Comanche Brave, Fort Reno, *1888, oil on canvas. Collection of W. B. Ruger*

school to assist in supporting his mother. He took a series of government jobs through family connections but was never content. Prior to his father's death, Remington had met Eva Caton. Eva, a student two years his senior, attended nearby St. Lawrence University. The two developed a close friendship, and Remington eventually proposed marriage. Eva's parents rejected the proposal because of his age and the fact that he had not yet established himself. Dejected, and frustrated with his career opportunities, Remington received family support to travel West, a dream which began during his years at Highland Military Academy. His family hoped such an adventure would encourage the young man to settle down. For several weeks in the late summer of 1881 Remington went to Montana. What he did is not known because no diaries, letters or art works are extant, save one image. Excited by what he saw there, Remington made and sent a crude sketch of cowboys and a scout to *Harper's Weekly*. Surprisingly, their editors had the sketch redrawn for publication in their February 25, 1882 edition (page 5). Because there was so much interest in the Southwest at that time, the editors saw no harm in retitling the work to *Cow-boys of Arizona — Roused by a Scout,* so that it would fit with an unillustrated article they wished to publish. Seen in hindsight, the editor's action is rather ironic.

Cow-boys of Arizona — Roused by a Scout, *wood engraving (redrawn by W. A. Rogers).* Harper's Weekly, *February 25, 1882. Arizona State Department of Library, Archives, and Public Records, Research Division, Phoenix*

The liberty taken by the editors because of heightened interest in the Southwest may have served as encouragement for Remington to explore the region. Following the Civil War adventuresome individuals cascaded west seeking fortune and fame. Few made it. Remington was no different, except he was encouraged to utilize the West as fresh material for the literate public. When he returned to New York in September 1881, he continued government office work to please his family, but he was preoccupied with another plan. On his twenty-first birthday Remington received his inheritance which freed him to pursue his dream. Through correspondence with a Yale friend, he arranged the purchase of a sheep ranch in central Kansas. Believing he would become a "gentleman rancher" with time to develop his art, Remington relocated. Faced with the labors of building a business in a frontier setting, he quickly realized his mistake and sold out, moving to Kansas City. There he invested in a couple of businesses and contacted Eva with good news of his success. He led her to believe his energies were being spent in a prospering iron brokerage business. Encouraged by his success, the two were married in 1884. They took up residence in Kansas City, however fortune did not shine upon the couple because Fred's business was not a brokerage. He was the silent partner in a bar which shortly went out of business, taking all of the young man's money with it. He had felt this arrangement would allow him to pursue an art career which is what he was doing in secret. Disgruntled, Eva returned home telling her husband that such an arrangement could not sustain their marriage. Down to his last few dollars, Remington headed for Arizona early in 1885 with the intention of documenting the richness of the diverse cultures there. He was especially drawn to the Indian Wars for which the reading public was enthralled. He was convinced he could make a name for himself through his art.

(Detail)
Standing Figure (Texas), *c. 1893, pencil on paper. Frederic Remington Art Museum, Ogdensburg, New York*

His efforts were rewarded. Upon his return, Remington met J. Henry Harper, publisher of *Harper's Weekly*, who hired him on the spot to provide illustrations of events in the Southwest. This initial success allowed the family to gain confidence in his career choice and Eva rejoined him. His abilities matured rapidly. In 1888 he won major awards at the National Academy of Design where he became an associate member in 1891.

Throughout the '90s Remington gained fame, but concurrently, the cavalry and Indian life he capitalized upon dwindled. Recognizing his dilemma, the artist shifted his attentions toward sculpture and writing. Toward the end of the decade Remington became despondent, his interests no longer fitting those of the lay audience, which resulted in *Harper's* no longer requiring his talents. He began experimenting with new color techniques in his painting and pushed forward his career under the influence of colleagues who painted in Impressionist and Tonalist styles. By 1903 he began to exhibit annually with New York galleries, and by the time of his death, was accepted by the tough New York critics as an equal of such well-known painters as Childe Hassam, J. Alden Weir and Willard Metcalf. The controversy of his career — illustration versus fine art — had been won.

The past decade has brought Remington's art into the spotlight of another controversy. A new generation of historians such as Richard Slotkin,

Patricia Limerick and Donald Worster are re-examining the West and drawing conclusions as they relate to current societal issues including economics, gender, environment and race. Promoted during his lifetime as the realist of the West, Remington's work is facing new scrutiny as these dialogues are redefined through art exhibitions, books, catalogues and criticism. This process is a healthy one, and through projects such as the recent exhibition, *The West as America,* Remington will emerge as a more complex artist than previously understood. Unfortunately, some of the dialogue surrounding Remington is not being considered in an objective manner. Objectivity should be the goal of the historian and art historian. Several important writers present him as an artist who saw little of the "Old West," rather, it is felt, he experienced a region in full development under the control of Eastern industrialists and capitalists. It was these entrepreneurs who collected his art, thus the artist is viewed as a promoter of their now unacceptable methods. He is further accused of stereotyping the Native American as a marauding savage who should have been eradicated by the heroic cavalryman and rancher. By accepting this view, Remington's work becomes a mere fictionalization of the past as he understood it.

This interpretation of Remington's work, or many other western American artists, while partially true, is unbalanced and certainly not fair. Creating an inquisition a century removed from an artist's career and then categorically condemning that artist is not an objective act. Remington did not live west of the Mississippi River, but he traveled there on eighteen separate occasions totalling almost four years of accumulated time. A tremendous volume of primary materials was also sent to his New York studio. Individuals who have spent less research time than this in order to condemn him should take a more careful approach. Also, the geography and urbanization, particularly of the Southwest, could be termed "developing," but not fully developed. True, mining interests were rapidly developing in New Mexico, Arizona and northern Mexico during the 1880s and 1890s, but no other industry existed. Agricultural interests were begun to feed the military, creating the roots of cities such as Phoenix, named only in 1870. More interesting is the criticism of Remington's inclusion with industrialists and capitalists. Throughout his life he was an investor in stocks which took plunges during two recessions. His patronage is complicated to establish and needs further study. One must realize the artist's chief patron was the lay audience, subscribers to *Harper's, Collier's, Outing* and other magazines, which gave Remington his reputation and initial wealth.

Accusation of racism in Remington's art is perhaps the most difficult criticism to assess. Recent writers have termed the artist "racist," based on derogatory written statements in his letters and diaries. Upon extensive examination of Remington's total writings it might be more balanced to term his attitude on race, ambivalent, especially if one includes his visual imagery. Positive statements regarding Mexicans and black troopers can be found often in his letters and published writings. And, the depiction of the black American and Mexican cavalrymen was always created in a dignified manner. In fact, very few American artists included more black Americans or Mexicans in their work. Oddly, Albert Boime's solidly researched book discussing the development of black stereotypes, *The Art of Exclusion: Representing Blacks in the Nineteenth Century*, excludes Remington — a rather significant omission. To be objective, Remington's attitudes should be judged as they pertained to his times, not only how they relate to life a century later. This is not to say today's Americans cannot learn from the artist's shortcomings, but he should not be judged a failure by only applying late twentieth-century norms.

There is no question Remington viewed the Native American, especially the Apache tribes of the Southwest, as being adversarial to his prime interest in military subjects and the westering development of dominate American culture. His work of the 1880s and 1890s makes this point clearly. However, following 1900 when "his West" had disappeared, Remington assumed a more sympathetic posture toward the Native American as his work became more nostalgic. This shift should be better recognized, and taken into consideration when an overview of the artist's career is scrutinized.

Remington was truly a man of his times. He was an artist and writer whose reactions to southwestern life are more complex than previously understood. That his career figures prominently in many varied discussions, of art, of history and of popular culture bespeaks the importance of his art. "Frederic Remington's Southwest" documents a specific aspect of this important American artist's life and work, while at the same time encourages a continuing dialogue as to how his art relates to America's history and how it responds to other artists of his time.

Frederic Remington in Arizona, *late 1880s, photographer unknown. Frederic Remington Art Museum, Ogdensburg, New York*

Frederic Remington's Southwest

IMAGINE THE EXHILARATION twenty-four-year-old Frederic Remington, an aspiring illustrator, must have felt in the spring of 1886 when he was hired by the editors of *Harper's Weekly,* America's most read journal, to document their most intriguing story. The young artist was to travel to the harsh deserts of southwestern America to join in the search and re-capture of the Apache Chief, Geronimo. Even though his experience was limited, having published but four drawings, Remington was their selection because he had been to Arizona the year before, and he was available.

For several years Geronimo had been leading a band of Apaches in rebellion against the U.S. government because of their poor treatment by the military on the San Carlos reservation, located in the eastern Arizona desert. Geronimo's gallant and sometimes treacherous actions still live in the minds of anyone interested in the history of the American West. Credit for this can be given first to Remington, and second to the many films about the Indian wars made during the middle years of this century whose directors were influenced indirectly by Remington's images.

Remington had sold his earlier works to *Harper's Weekly,* in fact, two images reproduced in January 1886 had been commissioned by the journal, perhaps by J. Henry Harper himself. Remington's involvement with *Harper's* was unlike that of his colleagues, as his work had been presented directly to Mr. Harper, rather than one of Harper's editors. During the fall of 1885 Harper was anxious to find an artist familiar with Arizona in order to enliven their reports on Geronimo, and at precisely that time the young artist appeared, having just returned from his first trip to the region.

Sunday Morning Toilet on the Ranch, *1885, watercolor on paper. Collection of Charles R. Wood*

Harper recounted their meeting in his 1912 memoirs, "When the late Frederic Remington first appeared in our office he looked like a cowboy just off the ranch, which, in fact was the case. The sketches he brought with him were very crude but had all the ring of new and live material. In course of conversation with him he told me that his ranch life had proved an utter failure..."

It is possible that among the pictures shown to Harper were *Sunday Morning Toilet on the Ranch* (page 10), *Attack on the Supply Train* (page 15), *Cowboys on a Cattle Thief's Trail* (page 13) and *Signalling the Main Command* (page 19), two of which are inscribed "Arizona Territory" and all four are dated 1885. *Sunday Morning Toilet on the Ranch* is a carefully composed watercolor depicting the life of cowboys as they spend a casual moment talking, smoking, and shaving. The picture documents the simple needs of these men who spent most of their time outdoors. The overall success of

The Apaches Are Coming, *1885, pen and ink, wash and gouache on paper. Frederic Remington Art Museum, Ogdensburg, New York*

this genre scene, which Remington most likely experienced, when compared to the less successful, *The Apaches Are Coming* (page 11), published January 30, 1886, helps one make several observations about Remington's approach to his early drawings. The former is a calm genre scene, while the latter, his second published illustration, captures a moment of excitement and action. Both events could have occurred at the same location, given the simple adobe building and adjoining crude corral. In the accompanying article for *The Apaches Are Coming*, Remington, also the author, described this New Mexican ranch as "scarcely little more than a cattle station... all its appointments are of the rudest and most primitive order." He goes on to describe when the cowboy bringing his galloping horse to a halt, cries his warning. "It was too late for the escape of women and children or such men who despairingly stayed to defend them. The best mounted cowboy did what he could, and then rode his horse to death in bearing the news to the nearest settlement. All the rest fell into the hands of the utterly merciless." The author is delivering to the Eastern reading

Arizona Indians, *n.d., photograph by Putnam and Valentine, Los Angeles, California. Frederic Remington Art Museum, Ogdensburg, New York*

public the exact Native American stereotype which had been personified in the press for some time. Remington, in his enthusiasm to please his publishers, invented a very expected image.

Technically, *The Apaches Are Coming* is inferior to the other Arizona scene. The articulation of the figures is awkward, the composition is not unified to the action and the space each figure occupies is not clear. This may be because the illustration was invented, while the ranch scene experienced. Throughout his career, Remington's most successful work was from models and direct experience. In this case, the work was commissioned in New York and more telling, the setting is borrowed from a photograph in the artist's own collection. (page 12, The author would like to recognize the staff of the Frederic Remington Art Museum for making this discovery.) The image is one from an entire photographic series, titled "Arizona Indians," made by Putnam and Valentine of Los Angeles, and its use sets a pattern for the utilization of photographs as preliminary sketch material by Remington during the early years of his career, a characteristic typical of illustrators and other artists.

A second quality of *The Apaches Are Coming,* which was a paradigm for Remington, was pushing the adversarial Apaches outside the picture. He emphasized the impending danger through the apparent defenselessness of the family as represented by the Madonna-like mother with child, her husband, their older daughter, an elderly gentleman (grandfather) and a reclining Mexican ranchhand. Remington's depiction of the Mexican is ambiguous in this picture because the aforementioned helpless figure is juxtaposed against the brave vaquero, the hero of the story.

Remington's lack of training, obvious in *The Apaches Are Coming* was no doubt apparent to the artist himself. He need only have compared his limited abilities with those of *Harper's* better illustrators such as Rufus

Cowboys on a Cattle Thief's Trail, *1885, watercolor on paper. The Bill and Irma Runyon Art Collections, MSC Forsyth Center Galleries, Texas A & M University, College Station*

Zogbaum, Henry Farney, or Thure de Thulstrup. Having received this significant assignment to head west for *Harper's,* Remington may have quickly enrolled in the spring session at the Art Students League in New York City because he left on assignment within days of completing his brief studies there. Years later in an interview for *Pearson's Magazine* the artist uncomfortably recalled, "My first commission was from *Harper's Weekly.* I did a picture based on an incident of the Geronimo campaign... But let the poor thing rest. It was a very bad drawing. I would rather not have it dragged from its well-deserved obscurity."

During the late 1880s many of America's leading illustrators could be found in the informal classes of the Art Students League. Remington enrolled in a painting class taught by J. Alden Weir who was well-schooled in academic French methods. Remington also enrolled in a much needed life-drawing class, as well as a sketch class, an ability which would be important in the field. Peter Hassrick, the leading authority on Remington, has written that the young artist learned two other lessons while at the League. One was the ability to make color notes as is demonstrated in his

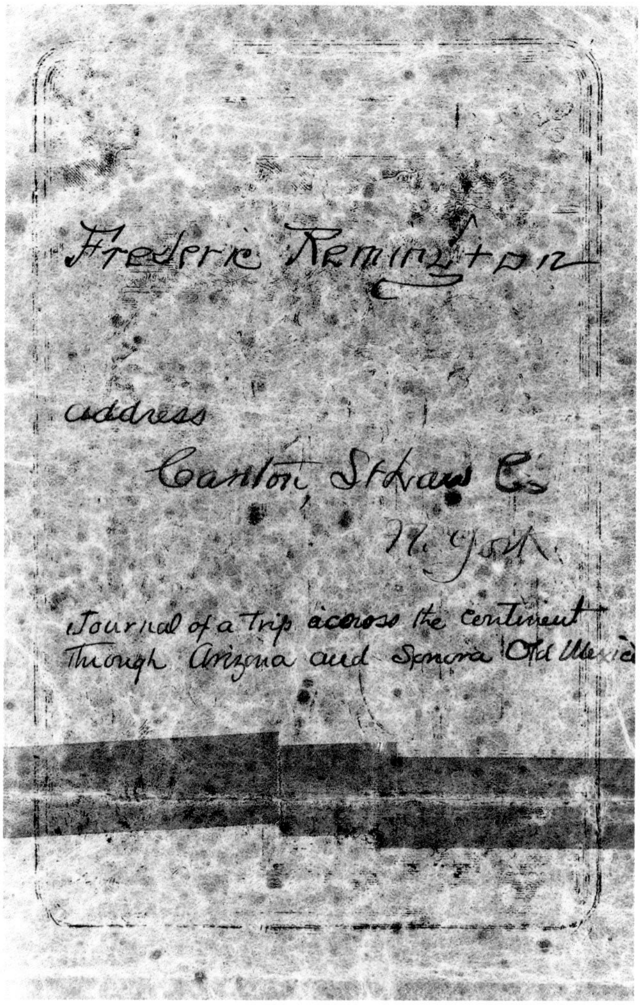

"Journal of a trip across the continent through Arizona and Sonora Old Mexico," *1886, pencil on paper. Robert Taft Collection, Kansas State Historical Society, Topeka*

journal of the 1886 trip, and the other was how to utilize the photograph as "sketch" material.

Remington titled the journal he kept on his western sojourn, "Journal of a trip across the continent through Arizona and Sonora Old Mexico" (page 14). His methodology to record his trip, which took place during June is somewhat odd for a visual artist. One would imagine, seeing the journal, that it was written by a reporter because of the interest shown in local phrases and quick observations of people and places. There are no sketches. Certainly there were other sketchbooks because of the proliferation of material to appear during succeeding months in *Harper's Weekly*, and also in *Outing* magazine, where over seventy pen and ink drawings relating to Arizona were reproduced over a five month period beginning in January of the next year. Three characteristics strike the reader of these journals, two of which are a follow-through from his brief time at the League. One was his consistent jotting of "color notes," or "c.n." which related to the landscape, "In the broken country of western [actually east-

Attack on the Supply Train, *1885, watercolor on paper. James R. Williams Trust*

ern] Arizona the earth is of a blue, red color — made cold in the shaddows [sic] and cold too in the sun though with marked difference. The misquit [sic] of a certain kind is a blue white green." He noted later, "Shaddows of horses should be a cool carmine and blue... There is a reflected light on a horse's belly." And, finally while he was briefly in Sonora, the painter observed, "It is impossible to get the white glare of the sun in this part. She [sic] cuts her lights square off and leaves no color in the high light but diffuses it all in one glaring mass though the shaddows from reflection are never dark and are always cold."

The reader of this important journal is also struck by the consistent mention of photography. During his train's layover in Deming, New Mexico, Remington apparently sought out a photographer. He noted, "Randall of Deming — photographer gave me two photographs." A few days later on June 10 in Tucson, Arizona Remington "Got up late after a good night rest at Palace Hotel took camera went to the detachment of 10th Colored Cavalry — took a whole set of photographs." Several days later at Fort Huachuca, Remington met Colonel Royal who assigned a trooper to the artist, "I photographed him in various attitudes and then made a quick watercolor. Also photographed a herd of government horses coming into Huachuca. Want now to get some photographs of the scouts." The importance of photography is again evident in the back of the journal where a list of photographed subjects is given and concludes with "38 views at San Xavier," the magnificent 18th century mission located in the desert just outside of Tucson.

In addition to the color notes, described picture possibilities and photography comments, this journal also records Remington's reactions to the

Texas, *c. 1893, pencil and ink on gray paper. Frederic Remington Art Museum, Ogdensburg, New York*

diverse people he met and places he visited. The entries are for the most part reportorial, attempting to serve as a reminder for possible pictures and articles. "I have just dined in a Mexican house. I am quite impressed by tortillas, frijoles I do not find enough... We ate in the tunnel between two houses — surrounded by dogs and hens in fact we contested the meal with them." Regarding a Mexican in Deming, Remington observed, "Saw vagabond setting on the platform with DeNeuville's (French military painter admired by Remington) Henry the 6th eyes very ferocious but not unduly agitated." On occasion his comments could be harsh, "The greasers are a vilinous [sic] looking set prone to moustaches and imperials. Their costumes are akin to the American tramp... They are a very degraded set."

Since he was under contract to join Lawton's troops in the hunt for Geronimo one would expect Remington to not be accepting of the tribes he saw. This is true of the Apaches, whom he did not actually see in action, but this is not the case of the Pimas and Papagos he observed around Tucson. He referred to the Papagos as "brave, industrious, sober, and chaste,... good horsemen, good with riatta (rope)." Remington saw the children being taught in school by one of the agents, "Bright children none knew any English two years ago and several understand a great deal."

When he was in Tucson, Remington also met and photographed the 10th cavalry, a black troop, referred to as Buffalo Soldiers. Little reference is made to them in his 1886 journal other than through a story of a daring rescue made of a black Corporal Scott by a white Captain, Powhatan H. Clarke. Making the acquaintance of Clarke, and pursuing the story of his heroics was to have a profound influence on Remington. The two became

Texas Cowboy, c. 1893, pencil on paper. Frederic Remington Art Museum, Ogdensburg, New York

friends and constantly corresponded until Clarke's accidental death in 1893. Clarke provided insights to the southwest and to the cavalry, and sent the artist photographs, uniforms, and Native American artifacts as study materials for use in his New York studio. "Lieut. Clark [Clarke is actual spelling]," Remington wrote, "is a young slim manly man and treated me cordially. Ordered the 1st serg[eant] to do anything for me." What convinced Remington of Clarke's character was the story of bravery the First Sergeant, a black, imparted to the artist while sharing a brandy. Remington was so taken by the story that upon his arrival at Fort Huachuca near the Mexican border, he sought out the wounded Corporal Scott in the fort hospital where he was recovering from the loss of one of his legs due to his wound. "The attendant led me to one [a bed] where a fine tall negro soldier lay. His face had a palor [sic] orspreading it the result of the lost limb. I greeted him pleasantly and told him of my desire to sketch his face... He narrated the event [his rescue] in simple soldierly language in the most approved negro dialect... 'all done got to shooting at the Lieutenant I tole him to drop me as we'd all be killed but he wouldn't do it no how!' I sketched his face, shook his hand heartily, and left him." Remington's re-creation of this rescue would be found two months later on the cover of the August 21 edition of *Harper's Weekly* (page 18), for the lead article "Soldiering in the Southwest." Clarke is shown, full face, being aided by a second, anonymous black soldier as they defy a barrage of bullets from the unseen Apaches. Scott appears dazed, with a wide-eyed expression, while Clarke remains calm under fire, his dapper white scarf blowing in the breeze.

"Soldiering in the Southwest" and similar articles such as "Plains Telegraphy" which appeared the prior month accompanied by *Signalling the Main Command,* evolved from Remington's decision once in Arizona not to pursue Geronimo because of the difficulties involved. Rather, he felt his talents

HARPER'S WEEKLY.

A JOURNAL OF CIVILIZATION.

Vol. XXX.—No. 1548.
Copyright, 1886, by Harper & Brothers.

NEW YORK, SATURDAY, AUGUST 21, 1886.

TEN CENTS A COPY.
WITH A SUPPLEMENT.

The Rescue of Corporal Scott, *wood engraving,* Harper's Weekly, *August 21, 1886. Arizona State Department of Library, Archives, and Public Records, Research Division, Phoenix*

Signalling the Main Command, *1885, watercolor on paper. James R. Williams Trust*

would be better spent recording the glamour and risks of the soldiers in this harsh, desolate environment. He made his feelings quite clear in this journal stating, "Let anyone who wonders why the troops do not catch Geronomo [sic] but travel through a part of Arizona and Sonora then he will wonder that they even try. Let him see the desert wastes of sand devoid of even grass, bristling with cactus, let the burning sirrocco [sic] fan a fever on his cheek, let the sun pour down white hot upon the blistering sand about his feet and it will be a plainer proposition... In all the world there is no such cheerless place, and the Indian for unknown generations have been reared and trained in this peculiar land." The artist's decision proved wise as it was several months before the Apache Chief was re-captured. Meanwhile, Remington had visited places, experienced cavalry life, and met individuals who were to provide him material for countless images throughout his career. In fact, it was this initial visit for *Harper's* and similar journeys during the next five years that allowed Remington to be viewed as an expert on the American and Mexican military.

Two years later, following the great success of his illustrations and published reports of the southwest, Remington returned to Arizona, this

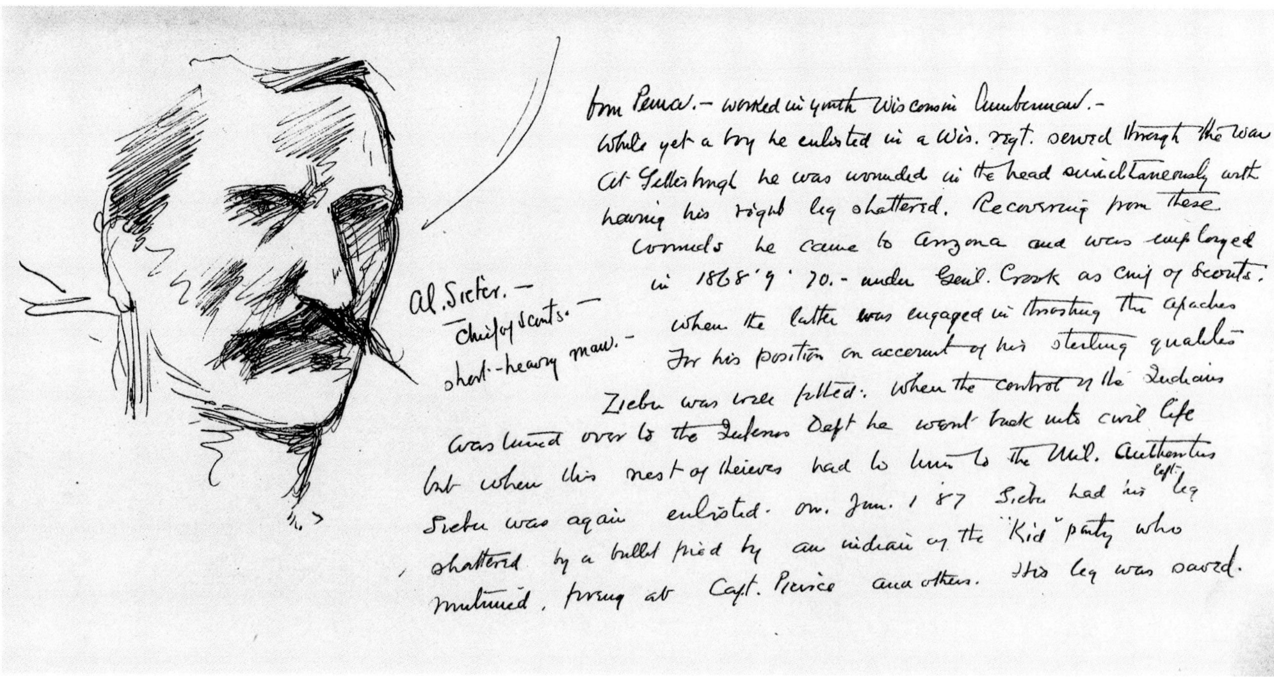

(Detail), Captain Albert Seiber, *n.d., pen and ink on paper. Frederic Remington Art Museum, Ogdensburg, New York*

time under contract to *Harper's* competitor, *Century Magazine. Century's* editors desired an illustrated article documenting the Buffalo Soldiers, and through Clarke, the artist had easy contact with the troops. Remington wrote to Clarke on April 11 prior to his departure, "I am going to do the 'Black Buffaloes' — this information you will please keep private as I do not want to be anticipated." Although the artist had paid little attention to this troop in 1886, Eastern readers found interest in their role in capturing Geronimo. Again, Remington kept a journal (page 21). Disembarking the train at Willcox, Arizona, Remington was met at Fort Grant the next morning by Powhatan Clarke "on horse surrounded by greyhounds — greeting very pleasant." Clarke, no doubt, had been pleased with the treatment Remington had given him in the magazine articles. From Fort Grant, Remington traveled with Clarke who told "many piculiarities [sic] which I hope to remember." Remington's second journal is more narrative than the first but similarly, contains color notations, photographic opportunities and other observations. During their scout, the observant Remington noted, "In Arizona nature allures with her gorgeous color and then repells [sic] with the cruelty of her formation — waterless, barren, and desolate... vast tiresome expanses and serrated peaks." On the 15th of June, while at the San Carlos Apache Indian Agency in east central Arizona, the artist "Got up early went down to the gathering after breakfast with — Captain V — photographed to my hearts [sic] content and the Indians never seemed to notice the camera." This is fascinating because he also notes the Apaches would not let him draw them. Again in this journal, verbal descriptions later became paintings, "was awake early and saw the

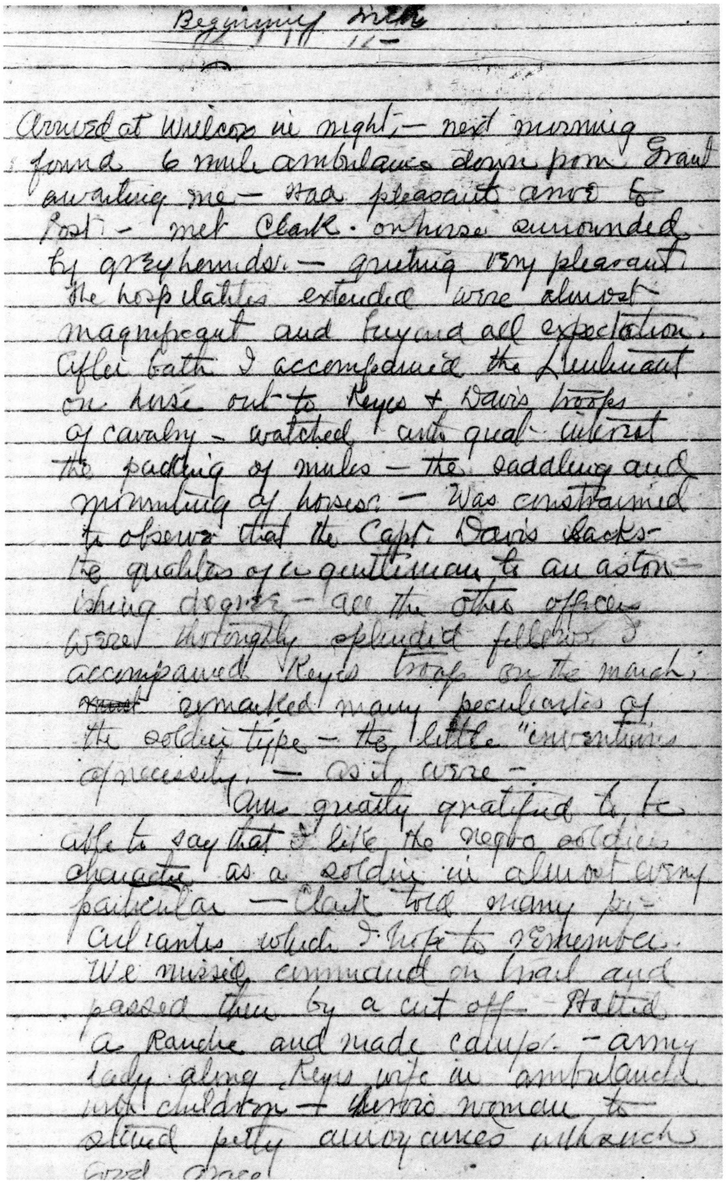
Beginning with

Arrived at Willcox in night — next morning
found 6 mule ambulance down from Grant
awaiting me — had pleasant drive to
Post — met Clark on horse surrounded
by greyhounds — greeting very pleasant.
The hospitalities extended were almost
magnificent and beyond all expectation.
After bath I accompanied the Lieutenant
on horse out to Keyes + Davis troops
of cavalry — watched with great interest
the packing of mules — the saddling and
mounting of horses — Was constrained
to observe that the Capt. Davis lacks
the qualities of a gentleman to an aston-
ishing degree — all the other officers
were thoroughly splendid fellows. I
accompanied Keyes troop on the march;
remarked many peculiarities of
the soldier type — the little "inventions
of necessity" — as it were —
Am greatly gratified to be
able to say that I like the negro soldier
character as a soldier in almost every
particular — Clark told many peculiarities which I hope to remember.
We missed command on trail and
passed them by a cut off — Halted
a Ranche and made camp. — army
lady along Keyes wife in ambulance
with children + heroic woman to
stand petty annoyances with such
good grace

Arizona, *1888, pencil on paper. Robert Taft Collection, Kansas State Historical Society, Topeka*

sun rise and day break — yellow, green, blue . . . lots of high color near the Earth — the soldiers stand about the camp fires and watch the breakfast cooking with a longing eye [see page 55]."

Unlike the 1886 journal, Remington's 1888 journal is less descriptive of people, speaking only of soldiers and officers. However, he did react initially to the Buffalo Soldiers, "I'm greatly gratified to be able to say that I like the negro soldiers [sic] character as a soldier in almost every particular." The published article was also more descriptive of the landscape and activities than it was about the Buffalo Soldiers themselves. A rare description of the black troop declared that to break the monotony of a long field maneuver, "officers have often confessed to me that when they are . . . troubled . . . of spirits, they have only to go about the campfires of the negro

Arizona Territory 1888 (or Marching in the Desert), *1888, oil on canvas (black and white). University of Wyoming, American Heritage Center, Gift of the Rentschler and Rita Cushman Families*

soldier in order to be amused and cheered by the clever absurdities of the men. Personal relations can be much closer between white officers and colored soldiers without breaking the barriers which are necessary to army discipline." Reading these passages over a century later, the language can seem patronizing, and it is true that in diary notes and letters Remington interspersed "negro" and "colored" with "nig" and "nigger." These comments and others have provided difficulties for recent writers about Remington's career. Matthew Baigell and John Russell, for instance, see Remington as a racist artist, but one must be cautious in overstating this characteristic which carries such a stigma. The reader and viewer of Remington's works should be careful in this area because the artist demonstrated proclivities on both sides of this tender argument. It is critical to look at the images made by the artist and then decide if he attempted to further these beliefs in an aggressive manner. Evidence throughout the artist's career will bear out that one cannot only condemn him. For every condescending description, a positive one can be offered in balance. In an article about a peccary hunt in Mexico, Remington wrote of one of his hosts, "The old fellow was very polite and dignified, as are all Mexican men." Back to the 1888 journal two entries read, "I witnessed an exhibition of American greatness today — a group — Chinaman Apache negro sol-

A Tumble from the Trail, *c. 1888, oil on board (black and white).*
Collection of Donald J. Sutherland, New York, New York

dier and white man." And more ambivalent, "These nigs are the best d(amned) soldiers in the world."

When published in April 1889, "A Scout with the Buffalo Soldiers" was accompanied by twelve illustrations depicting various actions described in the article. Both *Marching in the Desert* (page 22), also known as *Arizona Territory 88*, and *A Tumble From the Trail* (page 23), represent the band of soldiers Remington joined as they traveled hundreds of miles from Fort

Right hand page: Geronimo and His Band Returning From a Raid Into Mexico, *c. 1888, oil on canvas (black and white). From the Collection of Mr. and Mrs. M. Pfeffer*

Grant to Fort Thomas to the San Carlos Indian Agency and back. Their trek took them through the desert and over rugged mountains with few supplies. *Marching in the Desert* shows Clarke at the head of their cavalcade followed by Remington, hatted by the standard army summer pith helmet, and then the troopers. Remington wrote, "If the impression is abroad that a cavalry soldier's life in the southwest has any lawn party element in it, I think the impression could be effaced by doing a march... clouds of dust choke you and settle over horse, soldier and accoutrements until all local color is lost and black man and white man wear a common hue." In contrast, the same troop is shown from the rear in *A Tumble From the Trail* in order to better capture a disruption from the tedious march up a mountain. Remington recalled, "... suddenly with a great crash some sandy ground gives way and a collection of hoofs, troop-boots, ropes, canteens, and flying stirrups goes rolling over in a cloud of dust... the dust settles and discloses a soldier and his horse."

These two works demonstrate Remington's intent as an illustrator, and his understanding of the process of illustration. The images are simple, linear and minimal in color (actually painted in grisaille, or black and white). Each figure can be seen in outline form, the space is easily definable and outside of the main focus, detail is minimized. The event depicted is easily understood and relates directly to the accompanying text. Remington and other artists making illustrations during the late 19th century often worked in black and white to make the job of reproduction more simple. Their pictures were submitted to wood engravers who carved the images into woodblocks to be reprinted in black and white. The less detail included and the more linear the drawing, the more accurate the craftsperson was to the artist's creation. Likewise, by working in black, white and gray, the painter made the decision for the craftsperson as to what value of gray would be required for faithful reproduction. Remington's success as an illustrator not only lay in the fact that he was a student of the process, but also in his ability to choose subjects which would be of interest to the reading public, those which gave a romantic impression of the southwest.

Remington's scout with Clarke during the summer of 1888 cemented their friendship. Clarke eagerly accepted the assignment to serve as the artist's "eyes" in the field. He gathered materials and wrote of his interests and insights. And Remington, in turn, lived up to his promise recorded in a letter to Clarke containing offensive language, "All I want is one good crack at your nigger cavalrymen and d(amn) your eyes I'll make you all famous. Do you know I think there is the biggest kind of an artistic pudding lurking in the vicinity of Fort Grant... Well write and be gracious. I have made up my mind that you are a correspondent worthy of any ones [sic] steel." Given the number of articles and pictures created during the next few years such as *Geronimo and His Band Returning From a Raid Into Mexico* (page 25), *Leaving the Canyon* (page 28), *Arrival of a Courier* (1887),

Remington

Cavalry in an Arizona Sandstorm (page 33), and Remington's masterpiece, *A Dash for the Timber* (1889), the artist certainly lived up to his promise.

His feelings for Clarke are best summed up in his visual interpretations of the young soldier. Beginning with the image of Scott's rescue during 1886, Clarke appeared in the illustrations accompanying "A Scout with the Buffalo Soldiers," in Remington's *The Arrival of the Courier* which gained him admission to the National Academy of Design in 1887, in

Powhatan H. Clarke, *1889–1890, oil on canvas. Frederic Remington Art Museum, Ogdensburg, New York*

Skirmish Line — Target Practice, 1889, *pencil, watercolor and gouache on paper. Private Collection, Courtesy Gerald Peters Gallery, Santa Fe, New Mexico*

a portrait exhibited at the Society of American Artists in New York, and as the frontispiece for Clarke's posthumous 1894 article, "A Hot Trail (*Cosmopolitan*, October, 1894)." Unfortunately, only the upper third of Clarke's full-length portrait is intact (page 26), the remainder was destroyed by fire several decades ago. Luckily it was published for an article, "Two Gallant Young Cavalrymen," Remington authored for *Harper's Weekly* (March 22, 1890). The article describes Clarke as being "adored by his men," riding "horses which no one else can," and being "one of those old-time kind of 'ride into battle with his life on his sleeve' soldiers." The painting represented Clarke as a slender, confident, intense soldier. His attire of fringes, beadwork, scarf, and folded back hat are certainly romantic, but even in letters to Clarke, containing caricatures of the soldier (page 29), this is the way the artist saw him. In addition, Clarke was most likely the inspiration for the hero in Remington's second bronze, *The Wounded Bunkie* created six years later. Remington was so enamoured with Clarke that he frequently

Leaving the Canyon, *c. 1889, pen and ink wash on paper. Gene Autry Western Heritage Museum, Los Angeles, California*

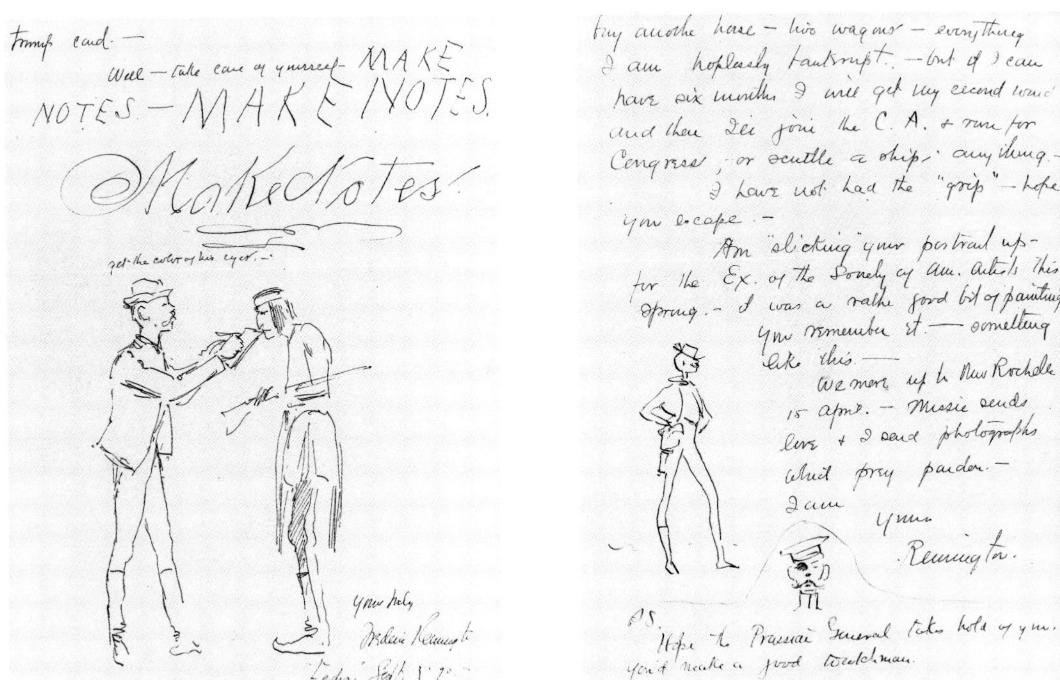

trump card.—

Well—take care of yourself—MAKE NOTES.—MAKE NOTES.

Make Notes!

get the color of his eyes.—

Yours truly
Frederic Remington
Sept. 1 '90

buy another horse—two wagons—everything
I am hopelessly bankrupt.—but if I can
have six months I will get my second wind
and then I'll join the C.A. & run for
Congress, or scuttle a ship: anything.—
I have not had the "grip"—hope
you escape.—

Am "slicking" your portrait up—
for the Ex. of the Society of Am. Artists this
spring.—It was a rather good bit of painting
you remember it.—something
like this.—

We move up to New Rochelle
15 April.—Missie sends
love & I send photographs
which pray pardon.—
I am
Yours
Remington.

PS
Hope the Prussian General takes hold of you.
You'd make a good watchman.

Two letters from Frederic Remington to Powhatan H. Clarke. Left: September 1, 1890. *Right:* September 30, 1890. *Missouri Historical Society, Powhatan H. Clarke Papers, Frederic Remington Letters*

Officers of the 10th Cavalry, Ft. Grant, Arizona, *c. 1890, photographer unknown. Powhatan H. Clarke is seated in the middle of the front row, flanked by Greyhounds on each side. Frederic Remington Art Museum, Ogdensburg, New York*

Lt. Carter Johnson, *c. 1889, watercolor on paper. Private Collection, Courtesy Graham Gallery, New York*

Lt. Carter Johnson, *c. 1889,*
watercolor on paper.
Mr. and Mrs. Jerry S. Handler

depicted other officers as if cut from the same mold. For example, in a later article for *Harper's Weekly* he described Lt. Carter P. Johnson as one of the hardest riders in the army and brilliant in his field maneuvers. The watercolor made of the lieutenant in the field (page 30) is one of Remington's most sensitive works ever created in the medium. Oddly, a second slightly larger watercolor was executed from the field sketch (page 31). Though not quite as sensitive to highlights and reflected light, it is almost identical, except for the brown scarf, which upon close examination is painted over the original striped one. One scenario for the existence of the second work could be that Remington, recognizing the quality of the piece did not want to risk its destruction at the hands of the wood engraver, which was normal due to the process of reproduction.

Am at work on a big oil — spring Academy or "Paris Ex" — dont know yet. "Lull in the Fight" — Sand hill — hot as devil — big plain · mesquit. Indians around in far distance. 4 old time Tex. cow punchers — one dead — two wounded — damnably interested — tough looking chaps. — four dead horses — saddles canteens, old guns buckskin &c — one man bandaging a damaged leg. — critics will give it hell — brutal — &c. — two characters. —

very rough — give you an idea. —

Two Characters, *from a letter dated December 27, 1888 from Frederic Remington to Powhatan H. Clarke. Missouri Historical Society, Powhatan H. Clarke Papers, Frederic Remington Letters*

Powhatan Clarke received a letter dated two days after Christmas, 1888, from Remington describing "a big oil... sand hill — hot as devil... Indians around in the distance. Four old time Texas cow punchers — one dead — two wounded... Four dead horses... one man bandaging a damaged leg — critics will give it hell — brutal." This verbal interpretation was followed by sketches of the main characters (page 32). The painting, *The Last Lull in the Fight,* now lost, was awarded the second class medal in the Paris Exposition, an exhibition whose American committee had rejected Albert Bierstadt's monumental picture of the West, *The Last of the Buffalo,* as being overly romantic. The baton had passed to a new image maker of the American West, an artist believed to be a realist. As

Cavalry in an Arizona Sandstorm, *1889, oil on canvas (black and white). Amon Carter Museum, Fort Worth, Texas*

a painter, Remington drew inspiration from several 19th century European military realists; Alphonse Marie de Neuville, Jean Baptiste Édouard Detaille, Ernest Meissonier, and Vasilii Vasilievich Vereshchagin, all of whom had tremendous, popular following. Excited by his recognition, Remington soon received his first commission. E.C. Converse desired a picture documenting the struggle of life and death on the frontier. Drawing on his southwestern experiences, his friendship with Clarke, and his inspiration from other artists, Remington created a scene viewed by most to be his southwestern masterpiece, *A Dash for the Timber* (Amon Carter Museum). A group of cowboys are shown beating their escape from a band of Apaches. Each cowboy can be seen as a different "type" and the frantic action of the horses was unlike any previous American picture. The masterful color nuances of the desert are exactly as the artist had recorded in his journals of the previous years. And, Clarke had provided details. On April 2, 1889, Remington requested of Clarke, "I want a lot of 'chapperras' — some two or three pairs — and if you will buy them I will be your slave. I want old ones — and they should all be different in shape...also that pistol holster which I left down there." These were to be utilized so that each cowboy would be different yet authentic to Remington's way of thinking. Shown in the fall exhibition at the National Academy of Design, *A Dash for the Timber* received many

Modern Comanche, *1890, oil on canvas. The Bill and Irma Runyon Art Collections, MSC Forsyth Center Galleries, Texas A & M University, College Station*

favorable responses from the critics. Remington believed he was no longer "just an illustrator" — he had arrived.

While Remington's painting *Last Lull in the Fight* was being lauded by the American jury for the Paris Exposition, he was on his way to Mexico with Thomas Janvier for *Harper's.* This trip was his fourth southwest sojourn in as many years for a major magazine, and would provide experiences for the finest series of illustrations he ever completed. Ironically, they were not for the commissioned project. As an accomplished author, and scholar of Mexico, Janvier should have relieved the pressure from Remington to have to look for stories as well as visual subjects. Left to concentrate only on the accompanying pictures, Remington was able to focus in a manner unlike his previous expeditions. Janvier's assignment was to produce a serialized story of ancient Mexico, "The Aztec Treasure House," for *Harper's Weekly.* Remington had difficulty creating the visual material and produced very poor illustrations for the article. One reason for this was the ancient world was totally unfamiliar to him and there was no primary material from which to work. The other, and perhaps main reason, was that Remington was intent on creating a series of major works on the Mexican Army. A clue to his interest can be found in an October 13, 1888 letter to Clarke at Fort Thomas, "Am full of work — just finished my 'Mexican Major' — great....Had heap of flattering things said about the large canvas. It has gone to Boston to be photographed." The conclusion of the letter includes several sheets of drawings for new U.S. military uniforms, some influenced by Mexican uniforms. It is not clear where Remington acquired his information for creating the "Mexican Major" because his only travels to Mexico at that time had been a few uncomfortable days spent in Hermosillo during the summer of 1886. In his journal only one entry related to the military, the remainder discussed the people and conditions. It is likewise not clear if this is *The Mexican Major* (page 36) published in Remington's own article for *Harper's Weekly,* September 27, 1890, long after the trip with Janvier. Remington's article opens with a description of the Mexican desert similar to his 1886 journal notes, "The scene is an arid upland in a white glare of sunlight...," and to add to the confusion, the picture is inscribed "copyrighted 1889" around the painter's signature. The painting was an atypically large size for Remington, which leads one to believe it is the "large canvas" to which Remington referred in his letter to Clarke. The only other possibility would be that he was discussing *A Dash for the Timber.*

Remington's focus on the Mexican army is confirmed by another letter to Clarke written on March 14, 1889, "My dear Clark [sic]," it opens, "I am just home from the City of Mexico where I have been doing the army. They are unusually picturesque and I have some good subjects. In your next letter write me all the facts you know concerning the operations of the Mex regular troops in Sonora — their methods — their marching and fighting — I may use it in connection with an article." No mention is made to Clarke of Janvier or "The Aztec Treasure House." According to Remington's biographers, Peggy and Harold Samuels, the artist had also arranged with the Minister of War to have available as models one representative from each area of the military as they traveled. For Remington to have made his trip with alternative mo-

Mexican Major, *c. 1889, oil on canvas. The Art Institute of Chicago, George F. Harding Collection*

tives was not unique, as two years earlier he had shifted from covering the Geronimo search in favor of recording the U.S. Cavalry.

The journal Remington kept opened in a fashion similar to the one he carried in the desert southwest the year before. Immediately his preconceptions are jolted upon entering the City of Mexico, as it was known a century ago. "The people are more fantastic than I imagined. The leather clothes — the diminutive burro. . . ." And several pages later the artist erupts in a rich passage which demonstrated the wealth of imagery he felt about him and how quickly he conceived what he wanted. In fact, four paintings for eventual articles are indirectly described.

> Gentlemen of the city only wear the national costume when in the saddle — it is often gorgeous there — rural people parade in their best — saw a regiment of Mex soldiers pass on the street (page 37). The drum and bugle corps played a familiar call (page 38) — and with long strides and swinging arms the soldiers marched along . . . they are terrible marchers . . . they are little men very brown — and their dirty canvas clothes are more picturesque than pertentious [sic] soldier that I was sketching (the ___ of the Engineers) (page 39) fainted as he was posing.

Troops in Mexico City, *1891 or 1893, photograph attributed to Frederic Remington, Frederic Remington Art Museum, Ogdensburg, New York*

In contrast to inventing the images for Janvier's project on ancient Mexico, the army provided Remington the real subject he desired. Only one aspect of the artist's plan went awry. When the article was proposed by Remington, Janvier received the commission because he was the Mexico expert. Fourteen images by Remington accompanied Janvier's article which came out in the November, 1889 issue of *Harper's Monthly Magazine*. The *Monthly*, unlike the *Weekly*, was published for an upscale audience, on glossy paper, more in book form and scale. Therefore its impact was seen to be more important. Of the fourteen reproductions nine were made from oil paintings in a new reproductive technique which actually hinted at the impasto in the painting's surface. *Drum Corps, Mexican Army*, the *Mexican Engineer* and *The Gendarme* (page 40) are superb examples of Remington's efforts. The *Drum Corps* captures the action to which Remington referred, and he carefully addressed the bright light and how it fell across the street and through the dust being kicked up. He used his standard right to left action which increased the sense of movement for the reader, whose eyes moved in the opposite direction across the magazine page. Also, the artist created a smaller stage for the action by closing in the composition with the buildings. Looking at *The Mexican Engineer* with all of his equipment and woolen uniform, it is easy to understand why this might be Remington's model who fainted. The artist utilized a standard portrait format in this picture and others for the series, but the confident painting quality sets them apart from his earlier, more linear pictures. The blending of colors in this series demonstrates a great step forward for Remington. By using the decaying architectural backdrop, he adds a painterly decora-

Drum Corps, Mexican Army, *1889, oil on panel. Amon Carter Museum, Fort Worth, Texas*

tion to the pictures. But when illustrated, the sensitivity and softness of the artist's touch and the gentle palette of the painting was lost. Janvier and Remington also produced smaller stories for *Harper's* as a result of their trip. *Bullfight in Mexico* (page 42) was a double page spread describing in detail the traditional Spanish sport, and for a superficial travel piece describing Mexican architecture, *Mexican Doorways* (page 41) was created and published two years later. Janvier refers so frequently to "Mr. Remington's drawing" that one assumes Janvier wrote the article from Remington's work, not the normal artist-writer relationship.

Fueled by the success of this 1889 trip, Remington's interest in Mexican subjects remained strong for several years. Returning there during 1891, 1893, 1896, and 1904, he wrote several articles. Examination of his southwestern itineraries make it clear that Remington viewed the entire territory from Fort Sill to Mexico City as "his area." This is particularly evident in the works he was commissioned to create for a series of articles by Colonel Theodore Dodge, "Some American Riders" (*Harper's Monthly*, published in successive months during the summer of 1891). *Modern Comanche* (page 34), *The Mexican Vaquero* (page 44), and *A Gentleman Rider*

Mexican Engineer, *1889, oil on canvas. Frederic Remington Art Museum, Ogdensburg, New York*

The Gendarme, City of Mexico, *1889, watercolor on paper. Museum of Fine Arts, Houston, Texas, The Hogg Brothers Collection, Gift of Miss Ima Hogg*

Mexican Doorways, *1891, pen and ink wash on paper. The University of Arizona Museum of Art, Tucson, Gift of Mr. and Mrs. Harry L. Bell*

on the Paseo de la Reforma (Private Collection), are the major pieces for this series. Remington's faithful likeness of a vaquero has little of Dodge's described qualities. Dodge wrote of the vaquero as generally being "a peon, and as lazy, shiftless, and unreliable a vagabond as all men held to involuntary servitude... he is essentially a low down fellow in his habits and instincts... a tinsel imitation of a Mexican gentleman." The vaquero provided by the painter for this article and many others he created was much different than the one Dodge put forth. Dodge and Remington were more in agreement on the Comanche Rider, which Remington chose to paint in a more romantic style. Wind whipping through the horse's mane, it is mounted by a rider looking off to the horizon rather than confronting the viewer, as was *The Vaquero*. Comanches, observed Dodge, know "more about horses than any other Indian. He is particularly wedded to and apt to ride a pinto (painted or piebald) horse, and never keep any but a pinto stallion." The artist's own diary entries are very similar to Dodge's report.

Many sketches of Mexico exist in the artist's archives at Ogdensburg, but it is difficult to identify on which trip various sketches were made. One group, made on blue toned paper, depicting a *Chicken Man* (page 43), a *Bread*

Bullfight in Mexico, *1889, oil on canvas. Santa Barbara Museum of Art, California, Gift of Mrs. Sterling Morton to the Sterling Morton Collection*

Man (page 43) and a *Padron* (page 43) among others, may date as early as the 1889 trip. Drawings of similar subjects appeared in Remington's own article for *Harper's Weekly* of December 12, 1890, titled "Mexican Burden Bearers." The refined sketches capture general attitudes, information and shading with some detail. The method was obviously quick due to the economy of line, but the completeness gives one the feeling that these sketches were intended to generate a finished drawing or painting.

The above statement would not hold true for the sketches Remington made on the Soledad ranch in Coahuila, Sonora, several years later. These sheets (page 46) reflect the artist's brief notations made at a ranch rodeo. He then had to depend upon his memory to utilize the material at a later date. Gone is Remington's written approach as seen through earlier journals. Rather, sketches and words are combined to be used for more finished work. A vaquero seen to the right in a brief sketch inscribed, "Soledad Ranch," is transcribed as a rider on the far left in the illustration created for

Top left: Bread Man, Mexico, *c. 1893, pencil on blue-toned paper*

top right: Chicken Man, Mexico, *c. 1893, pencil on blue-toned paper*

bottom: (Detail) Padron, Mexico, *c. 1893, pencil on gray paper*

all drawings Frederic Remington Art Museum, Ogdensburg, New York

The Mexican Vaquero, *1890, oil on canvas. The Art Institute of Chicago, George F. Harding Collection*

Cavalryman of the Line, Mexico, *1889, oil on canvas. Amon Carter Museum, Fort Worth, Texas*

the article Remington wrote, "The Soledad Girls (*Harper's Round Table*, May 4, 1897)." The finished illustration, *The Half-wild Cattle come Down From the Hills* (page 47) captures the moment an entire herd of cattle was brought in for the vaqueros to separate. Remington also produced an oil painting, *Vaquero, Soledad Ranch* (page 48), most likely intended to be reproduced in conjunction with the article. A passage from the story describes this work, "The rough and ready American range boss sat sideways in his saddle and thought — for he never talked unnecessarily, though appreciation [for the Soledad girls cowboying abilities] was chalked all over his pose." This pas-

(Detail),
Soledad, Mexico, *1896, pencil on paper. Frederic Remington Art Museum, Ogdensburg, New York*

Soledad, Mexico, *1896, pencil on paper. Frederic Remington Art Museum, Ogdensburg, New York*

The Half-wild Cattle come Down From the Hills, *1896, pen and ink wash on paper. Phoenix Art Museum, Arizona, Carl S. Dentzel Collection*

sage also points to an error in titling this picture, because the cowboy is obviously non-Hispanic given his dress and blond hair. The painting's inscription of "Soledad Ranch, Mexico" no doubt created this misnomer. He may even be the same individual seen in a photograph still in the Remington archives (page 49). As is typical of Remington's work, the subject dominated the picture plane while the elevation of the landscape created the stage on which the subject exists. Also standard is the use of minimal detail in identifying the location.

Vaquero, Soledad Ranch, Mexico, *c. 1896, oil on canvas. Maricopa County Historical Society, Desert Caballeros Western Museum, Wickenburg, Arizona*

Vaquero, Mexico, *1891 or 1893, photograph attributed to Frederic Remington. Frederic Remington Art Museum, Ogdensburg, New York*

Travels in Mexico always involved companions for Remington. He traveled with Janvier in 1889 and was the guest of General Nelson Miles two years later. In 1893, his publisher, Will Harper, accompanied him, and his final 1890s excursion included his friend Jack Summerhayes. The Miles trip resulted in an article extolling the virtues of Miles who constantly used the media to promote his career. Remington's trip with Harper was quite different. Their intent was to gather material for articles and paintings. They visited the Chihuahua Ranch of Jack Follansbee, a friend of William Randolph Hearst, whose ranch, Bavicora, adjoined Follansbee's. At the time, an abortive revolution was in the making, providing great material for a man like Remington. Life on the ranch was described in an article titled, "An Outpost of Civilization (*Harper's Monthly,* December, 1893)" and the military uprising was documented in two pieces for *Harper's Weekly,* "The Uprising in Chihuahua (May 6, 1893)" and "The Rebellion in Northern Mexico (December 30, 1893)." The most ambitious painting created was to accompany the latter article and depicted *The Revolution in Northern Mexico — Marching Regulars to the Front* (page 50). The composition of this work, capturing scores of troops, is quintessential Remington. The "V" configuration of the riders moves right to left across the canvas, in a completely void landscape of only dirt and clear blue sky. The articulation of the horses is superb and Remington chose to echo the white caps of the enlisted men in the white "boots" of their horses. Why Remington created such an ambitious work for this article is made clear in the minutes of the Officers Club at Fort Grant on September 11, 1894, "Whereas: A painting, in oil, entitled 'Revolution in Northern Mexico Marching Regulars to the Front,' having been presented to this Club by its distinguished artist. . . it shall be always carefully kept in an appropriate

Mexican Cavalry on the Move (or Revolution in Northern Mexico — Marching Regulars to the Front), *1893, oil on canvas. U.S. Cavalry Museum, Department of the Army, Fort Riley, Kansas*

place on the walls of this Club, not alone by reason of its peril as a painting... (because)... more than any other civilian [Remington] has by his art and kind sympathy, brought the United States Army to the favorable notice of the citizens of our country." The Officers Club took almost a year to so recognize the artist's generosity. In a letter from Remington to his friend, Owen Wister, written during the fall of 1893 (page 51) Remington boasts, "I sent an [sic] 'ile (lil') paintin — Mexican cavalry to Grant — officers mess — nice of me, wasn't it?"

The most demanding illustrative drawing Remington created as a result of his trip to Chihuahua was *Mexican Vaqueros Breaking a Bronc* (page 52), a large wash and watercolor not published until 1897 in Remington's picture book, simply titled, *Drawings.* The drawing, undated, is one of Remington's finest efforts in the medium and can be assumed to have been based on the ranch as its description fits the picture. The brand, so prominent on the foreground horse, combines the letters "H" and "F" which could stand for Hearst and Follansbee. As neighboring American ranchers in Mexico, and close friends, perhaps they ran their cattle together.

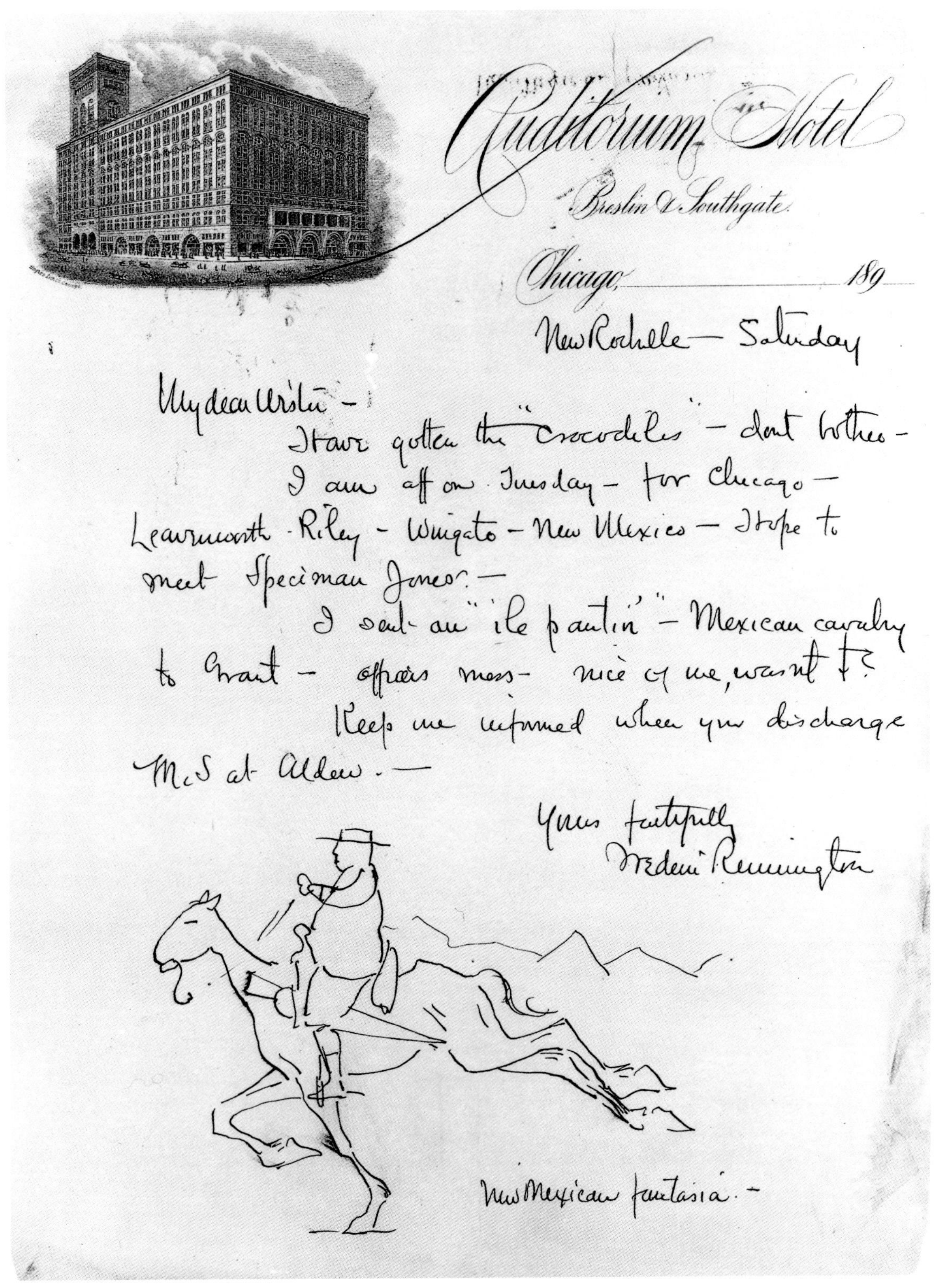

Auditorium Hotel

Breslin & Southgate.

Chicago, 189

New Rochelle — Saturday

My dear Wister —

I have gotten the "crocodiles" — dont bother —

I am off on Tuesday — for Chicago —

Leavenworth - Riley - Wingate - New Mexico — I hope to meet Specimen Jones. —

I sent an "le pantin" — Mexican cavalry to Grant — officers mess — nice of me, wasnt I?

Keep me informed when you discharge McS at Alden. —

Yours faithfully

Frederic Remington

New Mexican fantasia. —

Letter from Frederic Remington to Owen Wister, *written on Auditorium Hotel Stationery, c. 1894. Manuscript Division, Library of Congress, Washington, D.C.*

Mexican Vaqueros Breaking a Bronc, *1897, pen and ink and wash drawing. Museum of Fine Arts, Boston, Massachusetts, Bequest of John T. Spaulding, 48.874*

By the turn of the century Remington's interest in Mexico had waned. Among his last works depicting the area was one for an article about a troop of volunteers, "The Honor of the Troop (*Harper's Monthly*, July, 1899)." It tells the story of a group of volunteers competing with other troops to capture three bandits. Through the help of nine Mexican "scouts" they succeed as is shown in *Interrogating Mexican Bandits* (published as "The Three Bandits were led back into the Path," page 53). The nostalgic tenor of the article indirectly proclaims the end of the artist's passion for Mexico as a subject for his work.

Viewing Remington's accomplishments for the decade, the paintings and drawings of Mexico showed a very capable, dignified military organization. His approach to the vaquero was practically as an equal to his American counterpart, the cowboy, an evolution Remington well understood. The poverty which he observed and noted in his journals rarely interested him in his published work. Remington knew his audience well. He also understood the needs of his patrons, and those of the publishers' to meet the demand of their readers.

Interrogating Mexican Bandits (or The Three Bandits Were Led Back into the Path), *1899, pen and ink wash on paper.*
Mr. and Mrs. William Healey

The acclaim Remington received for his easel painting efforts of 1889, *Last Lull in the Fight* and *A Dash for the Timber* encouraged the painter to continue similar efforts in addition to his illustrated articles for significant national publications. The burning desire for fame and fortune which he had as a student had not subsided. Remington consumed life as did so many Victorian men. His heavy travel schedule and high living style with friends at private New York clubs can be paralleled in the lives of countless other individuals. If one were to compare Remington to any other well-known person of his day it would be Theodore Roosevelt, who was the paradigm of the "strenuous life," as he termed it. The two were acquaintances and later in the decade, following the Spanish American War, Remington would commemorate the "Hero of America" in paint. Prior to the rampant technological advances of the early twentieth century, an individual was still able to approach life with the goal of being a "renaissance man" of sorts, thus Remington's desire to paint, report, illustrate, write short stories, eventually novels, and make important sculptures.

Remington knew he embellished the lives of those he depicted in his art. It did not concern him that at the same time he was touted as the "realist" of the West. A century later it is difficult to understand this conflict, and what was then viewed as harmless by the creator is interpreted as harmful by the critic. It has been pointed out that the officers of the Army saw Remington as their great promoter. For the generation following the Civil War, military men were honored with political appointments, unearned titles, and even monuments. Well into the 1890s public displays of gratitude were still proliferating for Civil War heroes. To those men still in the military, little attention was given them, except for their heroics though the Indian Wars. Since Remington's own father had been a local war hero and died rather young, following his son's graduation from a military academy, the artist's interest in the military was no surprise. That he honored the cavalry and infantry was to be expected. Remington's longing to participate in similar action leads one to interpret much of his work as a vicarious act, and explains his intense interest in every detail of military life. He thought heroes and heroics were crucial to understanding American life, a characteristic which has been lost a century later.

Remington also looked to the less exciting side of military life in his major works. The metaphor of a life and death frontier existence so apparent in his most popular images also had a more passive side. As had Winslow Homer in his Civil War subjects, Remington found gratification in showing the everyday existence of a soldier's life in the desolate reaches of America. *Cavalryman's Breakfast on the Plains* (page 55) and *Roasting the Christmas Beef in a Cavalry Camp* (page 56), completed about 1892, serve as tremendous examples. During Remington's travels in the southwest during 1886, 1888, and 1889, he experienced similar scenes and knowing his own proclivity toward good food, good drink, and good cigars, he no doubt was a frequent "campfire visitor." *Cavalryman's Breakfast on the Plains* could be termed a narrative, genre painting due to its everyday subject and the artist's device of making multiple vignettes within the painting. The dramatic recession of space and the masterful handling of atmospheric perspective tie the composition together beautifully. This compositional method was typical of other western illustrators who dealt with the great landscape expanse, and nowhere is this characteristic better demonstrated than in Homer's great 1871 painting, *A Rainy Day in Camp* (Metropolitan Museum of Art). Remington has closed his space down more than Homer by lowering the angle of the orthagonal line represented by the picketed horses. This enabled Remington to include four vignettes near the picture plane, unlike Homer who had but one group warming themselves around a morning fire.

Roasting the Christmas Beef in a Cavalry Camp could almost be viewed as a pendant to *Cavalryman's Breakfast on the Plains.* The Christmas picture was reproduced in *Harper's Weekly* as a double page seasonal picture with no supporting article, thus it was not technically an illustration (page 56). Having to stand alone, lacking the support of a text, the visual narrative is even more important and captured the total attention of the painter. Again a strong orthagonal is established, this time by a row of sibley tents and

Cavalryman's Breakfast on the Plains, *c. 1892, oil on canvas. Amon Carter Museum, Fort Worth, Texas*

a low ridge. Various activities occur throughout the camp, but real attention is given to the roasting of a special meal. Sharing the occasion and a "smoke" with the soldiers is an Apache scout. When reproduced in *Harper's* (page 56) the work was slightly altered. A distant mountain in the painting helps define the space, and the rider seen on the ridge in the *Harper's* version is a riderless horse in the painting. The rider has moved down the ridge to the center of the painted composition. Whether Remington repainted the work is not known.

When considering Remington's writings and his visual images, his attitudes about the peoples of the West seem ambivalent. Therefore, placing him in history, as historians and critics must, is not easy. Adding to the difficulty, other individual's beliefs have been credited to him because his images illustrated their articles. Critics will often point to the shared belief of artist and author when examining the text of articles, yet the relationship between written word and illustration is not always the marriage one would expect. Remington's work for the Janvier article regarding the Mexican Army, or the Dodge series, "American Riders" serve as examples. More

Roasting the Christmas Beef in a Cavalry Camp, *c. 1892, oil on canvas. Yale University Art Gallery, New Haven, Connecticut, Gift of Mrs. Dorothy Knox Goodyear Rogers in Memory of Edmund Pendleton Rogers*

Roasting the Christmas Beef, *wood engraving,* Harper's Weekly, *December 24, 1892. Arizona State Department of Library, Archives, and Public Records, Research Division, Phoenix*

An Incident on the March, *1891, pen and ink and wash on cardboard. The Carnegie Museum of Art, Pittsburgh, Pennsylvania, Andrew Carnegie Fund*

misunderstood when read today is an article such as "General Crook in the Indian Country" published by *Century* four months after the slaughter of the Sioux at Wounded Knee in December 1890. John Bourke, the author, was an aide to Crook throughout the 1870s and 1880s when the General was assigned to end the "Indian Conflict." Bourke's article is flagrantly anti-Indian and pro-progress, as defined by him, who "looked upon the bleak prairie touched by the wand of progress and [saw] great cities spring into life." Remington's dozen illustrations do not highlight Bourke's text, rather they include generic military imagery. One rather pointed drawing, *An Incident on the March* (page 57), of a dead soldier found by comrades is an exception. The lance stuck in the ground behind the fallen soldier is the clue to his death. Interestingly, the original wash drawing lacks the emphasis on the corpse the craftsperson put into the reproduction. A second watercolor reproduced with the Bourke article was *The Infantryman in Field Costume*

The Infantryman, *1890, watercolor on paper. Harriet Russell Stanley Fund 52.16, New Britain Museum of American Art, Connecticut*

Captain Dodge's Colored Troopers to the Rescue, *1891, tempera on paper. Mrs. Charles Steward Mott Collection, Courtesy of the Flint Institute of Arts, Michigan*

(page 58), a wonderfully articulated document, similar to the scores of drawings included in the artist's correspondence with Powhatan Clarke.

A more balanced article was written for the same magazine seven months later about a conflict between the 5th Cavalry and the Ute Tribe during 1879. The Utes had the upper hand in the battle until Captain Dodge of the 9th Cavalry brought his troop of Buffalo Soldiers to the rescue (page 59). He brought the conflict to conclusion without losing any of his men. Remington, drawing on his Arizona experience, chose in this instance to beautifully record the crux of the article, the frantic forward charge, which is more typical of an illustrator's role.

The demands for Remington's work during the early 1890s continued to increase. Scores of illustrations were commissioned. Remington's signature alone would sell magazines and books. He continued to exhibit paintings in major New York exhibitions, and in 1893 he organized his own sale at the American Art Galleries. At the same time Remington received strong attention to his work, his subject matter experienced an unnoticed erosion. The Indian Wars were declared over, and even the historian, Frederick Jackson Turner, in a paper delivered in conjunction with the 1893 World's Columbian Exposition declared the frontier closed due to the demographics of the West. It became more difficult for Remington to gain firsthand experiences. In order to keep his income steady, he began illustrating more fiction, nostalgic articles and eventually pulp novels. For Richard H. Davis's series "The West From a Car Window," published in *Harper's Weekly* over several issues during

Water, *1892, pen and ink wash and gouache on paper. Frederic Remington Art Museum, Ogdensburg, New York*

1892, Remington created an erratic group of works. Though technically sound, as can be seen in the portrait of *Captain Hardie* and *Water* (page 60), these works lacked the artist's previous verve. The picture of Hardie was drawn by Remington from a photograph for the article, and seemingly to make amends for doing so, the artist made a second, superb portrait of Hardie, inscribed with a different title, at a later date when the two met in Chicago (page 62). As was his manner, the artist presents a Clarke-like dandy of an officer. For Davis's segment on ranch life in Texas, Remington's illustrations took on greater significance, showing the active cowboy life he knew there. The first of the drawings for this article based on the King Ranch, was the beautifully animated *Pitching Bronc* (page 61). The fluidity of the washes contrasted by the strong linear outline of the bucking horse and its rider create a dramatic image, which the artist would explore during the next several years.

Two wash drawings from the mid '90s, one in black and white the other in color exemplify the extreme nature to which Remington's illustrations were being taken. One, *They Left Him Thar' in the Trail* (page 63), appeared as the frontispiece in Alfred Henry Lewis's 1895 pulp novel, *Wolfville*. It records the instant when the story's hero, Cherokee Hall, leaps from a stage traveling between Wolfville and Tucson, to hold off an entire renegade Apache band while the driver safely goes on to his destination.

A Pitching Bronc, *1892, ink wash on paper. Mrs. William A. Seifert, Jr.*

Lt. Hardie, *c. 1892, watercolor on paper. Frederic Remington Art Museum, Ogdensburg, New York*

They Left Him Thar in the Trail, *c. 1895, pen and ink wash on paper. Phoenix Art Museum, Arizona, Gift of Friends and Family in Memory of John W. Kieckhefer*

Holding Up the Pay Escort (or The Hold-up), *c. 1894, watercolor on paper. Valley National Bank of Arizona, Phoenix*

As fashion for such stories would have it, Hall was found later with several arrows lodged in his body but lived to tell his story. Remington draws on this moment to delineate the horses flying in action under the fury of a magnificently curvilinear whip. The second work, *Holding Up the Pay Escort* (page 64), provides a bit of intrigue. It was originally reproduced in conjunction with Owen Wister's short story, "A Pilgrim of the Gila," published for *Harper's Monthly* in November, 1895. A colleague of Remington's, Wister had visited Tucson during 1893 and 1894 to gather material for his story. The writer must have learned about the infamous Army pay wagon robbery of May 11, 1889, which resulted in a much talked about court action. At about the time of the event, Remington was a visitor to the area between Forts Thomas and Grant where the robbery took place. He may have heard the event recounted among the soldiers but it was not until Owen Wister wrote his short story that the image was published. Because of the controversial trial following the conviction of the robbers, the case was famous throughout the area. What is interesting is not that Wister used the event as a central theme in his story or that Remington created a delightful composition. Rather, when compared to an actual photograph of the holdup site, re-created by investigators the day after its occurrence, the artist's rendition is an exact report, down to the foliage (photograph, collection Arizona Historical Society). The artist's dependence on photographs, which had been limited for several years, now returned in order to hold on to the subject matter he saw slipping away.

Owen Wister and Remington first came together as writer and illustrator during the fall of 1893. They were quite a contrast. Remington was at the height of his fame, while Wister was a struggling writer of fiction. Wister was a slight man, Harvard trained, grew up in a main line Philadelphia family and initially went west as therapy of neurasthenia, a common diagnosis of upper-class victims of stress-related illnesses. His counterpart was a large, dominating figure, at that time weighing around two hundred forty pounds, who had worked hard to gain his station in life. Having just lost Powhatan Clarke as an inspiration for his art, Remington now adopted Wister to write articles for which he planned the illustrations. This, Wister did for a period of time, until his own career gained a following at which time he tried to extricate himself from dependence on Remington. Wister's reputation today rests solely on his famous book, *The Virginian,* published in 1902 which gave birth to the stereotypical cowboy — rough riding, hearty, honest, and independent. Less known is the tremendous influence Remington had in the early development of Wister's concept of the cowboy and the West. Throughout 1894 the painter had been pushing the writer to record the history of the cowboy in an article, continually feeding information to Wister through his letters. Eventually Wister published "The Evolution of the Cow-Puncher" (*Harper's Monthly,* September, 1895), for which Remington created five major oils to be included as illustrations. This work served as the paradigm for the Virginian years later. Unfortunately, Wister's being an Anglophile got the best of him, and he radically altered Remington's view of the cowboy to make the entire "evolution" one from Saxon heredity, not Mexican, as Remington advised. Wister's concluding summation paragraph began, "Such is the story of the cow-puncher, the American descendant of Saxon ancestors, who for thirty years flourished upon our part of the Earth, and because he is not compatible with progress, is now departed, never to return." Remington had asked for a reflection of a life he saw passing, but Wister's version is not quite what he envisioned.

While pushing Wister to complete his article, Remington made what was to become a tremendous breakthrough in his career. Disturbed by Wister's procrastination on completing the "evolution" the artist wrote to him in January, 1895, "Either leave the country — Manuscript or Die." But he then went on to explain in detail his own frustration as an artist and what he was doing about it, "I have simply been fooling my time away — I can't tell a red blanket from a gray overcoat for color." Though referring to his career as an illustrator, the artist also let out a secret.

> I have got a receipt [sic] for being great — everyone may not be able to use this receipt but I can. D[amn] your glide along songs — they die in the ear — your Virginian will be eaten up by time — all paper is pulp

now. My oils will get old wasting . . . my watercolors will fade — but I am to endure in bronze — even rust does not touch — I am modeling — I find I do well — I am doing a cowboy on a bucking broncho and I am going to rattle through all the ages, unless some Anarchist invades the old mansion and knocks it off the shelf (page 66).

my oils will all get old wasting - that is, they will
look like old molasses in time - my watercolors
will fade - but I am to endure in bronze -
even rust does not touch. - I am modeling -
I find I do well - I am doing a cow boy
on a bucking broncho and I am going to rattle
down through all the ages, unless some Anarchist
invades the old mansion and knock it off the shelf.

Letter from Frederic Remington to Owen Wister, *January 1895. Manuscript Division, Library of Congress, Washington, D.C.*

Remington's first bronze, *Bronco Buster* (page 68), copyrighted later that year, was based on the many photographs, experiences, and previous works he had produced, mostly from ranches in Texas and Sonora. His prediction to Wister came true, as his action packed sculpture was to become an icon of American art and the West, selling over one hundred casts during the artist's lifetime.

Remington's tremendous contribution to American sculpture has gone basically unnoticed, in part because so many reproductions and fakes have been available. One rarely sees the "real" Remington. Secondly, his reputation as an illustrator was immediately placed on this bronze and others. And more recently, when a fair judgment could have been made relative to a major 1989 retrospective, his career was enmeshed in the revisionist controversy of the factual West as interpreted today, not how he interpreted it. In comparing Remington's major bronzes created within the last fourteen years of his life to those made by his contemporaries and predecessors, one realizes no artist had ever captured action so successfully in three dimensions.

Except for the sketches made of antique casts at Yale during his eighteen months there, Remington developed predominately as a self-taught sculptor. Later, during 1894, he received what might be termed "on the job training" watching Frederick Ruckstull create the model for an equestrian monument in a neighboring studio. Actually, his lack of experience was an asset because he challenged the foundry to create the figure as he drew it, not in a manner which it could be built. This dialogue was to remain between the artist and the foundry throughout his brief working career as a sculptor.

In order to solve his requirements at the foundry, new methods were discovered for constructing armatures to produce the bronzes. Initially the foundryman felt it impossible to support the weight of the wildly bucking horse in such a top heavy, asymmetrical composition proposed for *Bronco Buster.* The cowboy, quirt in hand, remains atop the lunging horse by grabbing the mane and pressing his knees to the horse. With his feet almost free of the stirrups, there is an excitement created over who will be the victor, horse or rider.

Coming at a time when Remington was questioning his own future, *Bronco Buster* was a savior. During the next four years, he turned his attention to working "in mud" as he called modeling in clay, and to writing. Unlike his contemporaries, Remington stayed involved with the making of each sculpture. He did not merely ship off the model and receive the bronzes. He made frequent visits to the foundry, making changes in the details of different pieces such as arm positions, quirts, and in the *Bronco Buster,* years later, putting woolly chaps on the rider instead of leather. He continually strived to improve upon his own work. After reworking *Bronco Buster* over a ten-year period, Remington then undertook a similar bronze, *The Rattlesnake* (page 69), to apply what he had learned. A spiral of action from bottom to top in the latter composition encouraged the viewer to experience the frightened, lurching bronco from all angles. The line of action begins with the left rear hoof and proceeds along the sweep of the tail which is echoed by the horse's head, which twists to keep the feared snake in view. The cowboy strains to maintain his center of balance and accomplishes the same for the composition of the sculpture. This resolved the criticism of his first bronze in that it was conceived as a two-dimensional "illustration" in bronze.

Remington had quickly realized his shortcomings in reproducing one

Bronco Buster, *1895, bronze (Roman Bronze Works cast no. 7). Maricopa County Historical Society, Desert Caballeros Western Museum, Wickenburg, Arizona*

The Rattlesnake, *1905, bronze (Roman Bronze Works cast no. 48). Mr. William H. Brophy II*

The Outlaw, *1906, bronze (Roman Bronze Works cast no. 4). Private Collection, Paradise Valley, Arizona*

Wounded Bunkie, *c. 1896, bronze (Henry-Bonnard Co. Founders, unnumbered cast). Thomas Gilcrease Institute of American History and Art, Tulsa, Oklahoma*

of his famed broncs in metal. His second sculptural effort, *Wounded Bunkie* (page 71), was a much more complex undertaking. The artist chose one of his typical images of heroics from the southern plains and the southwest, but this time added a second horse which created a new problem of unifying separate entities into one composition. The frenzy of the officers beating their retreat is felt through only two of the horses' eight hoofs touching the ground, a tough problem for the foundry to solve. The horses turn in on each other as if assisting just as the one rider who supports his wounded bunkmate. The detail of this bronze and the various viewing silhouettes are memorable, capturing all the artist had to express. Unhappily, Remington symbolized the passing of the West by the buffalo skull which lies on the ground as an unnecessary footnote, even in his own time, to a great work of art.

Remington's homage to the cowboy which presented the greatest technical challenge to capture severe action was *The Outlaw* (page 70), created in 1906. The outlaw pony was so intent on removing the rider from its back that it assumes an almost vertical position leaping into the air and violently kicking up its rear hoofs. Remington wanted to catch the action at the instant the horse left the ground. The cowboy is so intent on staying aboard, he grips his hand into the side of the horse. In a Christmas card to Riccardo Bertelli, the owner of Roman Bronze Works and his collaborator in invention, Remington drew a caricature of himself and Bertelli looking at the clay on the modeling stand. Remington is shown to ask, "Can you cast him?" and the foundryman's retort is, "Do you think I am one of the Wright brothers?" The success of this work is that finally Remington had captured what was easy in paint, or photography but nearly impossible in bronze.

Shifting his artistic attention toward sculpture beginning in 1895 had helped Remington to intellectually address how he could deal with the fading subject matter of the West upon which he had built his reputation. Dealing with a new material, in a manner never before approached, helped to divert attention that might otherwise have proven problematic. In a similar vein, the outbreak of war with Spain in Cuba during 1898 gave Remington the war he had always desired to record. Sent by Hearst and *Harper's* to Cuba, the artist's romantic notions of war were shattered. The unbelievable carnage of war and the conditions in Cuba literally made Remington ill. What he experienced completely distorted his vision of war, given he had felt battle to be almost an honored, gentlemanly sport. Following his return, the artist was practically unable to work, his self-esteem wavered and he sunk into despair. Overindulgence forced his weight to two hundred ninety-five pounds.

The popular national image of the cowboy and the cavalry at the end of the 19th century had been developed for the most part by one individual, Frederic Remington. However, these subjects which he had tackled head-on during the century's final decade had passed him by. Metaphorically, an 1898 painting such as *The Pursuit* (Virginia Museum of Fine Arts) demonstrates this notion. The painting's point of view is far to the rear of the pursuing cavalry and the artist (viewer) is challenged to keep pace. This painting which accompanied a fictionalized story, "The Essentials of Fort Adobe (*Harper's Monthly*, April, 1898)" is the same for Remington. He was confronted with maintaining a dream of a West and Southwest which had previously existed for him. He was one of America's best known artists with a drive toward fame and success. He had lived for years on the popularity of his illustrations while trying to be accepted as a fine artist. By the final years of the last century, Frederic Remington was at a crossroads in his career, unsure of what direction to pursue.

Though his West had vanished, Remington found a solution to this crisis. The resolution was played out during the final decade of his life, the first decade of the twentieth century. Whereas his subject had retreated into history, he refused to let it go entirely. Moving from his reportorial approach to a more nostalgic position regarding cowboys, the cavalry and

Army Mule with Harness Marks, *n.d., oil on canvas. Buffalo Bill Historical Center, Cody, Wyoming, Gift of the Coe Foundation*

especially Native Americans, he resolved to be judged, stylistically, with painters of his own generation who were respected as modern painters. Their styles centered on Impressionism and Tonalism.

Remington went West to Colorado and New Mexico, in 1899 and 1900, hoping to find a new approach to "his" subject matter. He had to solve his use of color which is evident in a letter he wrote to Howard Pyle, the well-recognized illustrator, "Just back from a trip to Colorado and New Mexico. Trying to improve my color. Think I have made headway. Color is great and it isn't so great as drawing and neither are in it with imagination. Without that a fellow is out of luck." Several months earlier Remington must have outlined his personal dissatisfaction to Pyle (Remington letter lost) because the latter's response is rather telling. He wrote with sympathy to Remington of "a feeling that somehow you were not happy in your heart. I agree with you that one cannot be entirely successful when one departs

Untitled (adobe pueblo with baking oven), *c. 1900, oil on board. Buffalo Bill Historical Center, Cody, Wyoming, Gift of the Coe Foundation*

out of one's line of work." These remarks are then followed by words of encouragement, "Your line of work is very strong... you do not know how many admirers you have..."

Within months Remington was again in the New Mexico area visiting Ouray, Colorado, Santa Fe, Taos and other locations. He met Bert Phillips, a founder of the Taos art colony. During his trip the two discussed painting, and it is from these trips that oil sketches such as *Untitled* (adobe pueblo with baking oven) (page 74) were probably executed. This fresh painting, depicting Taos pueblo, was indeed a departure for Remington, in its rapid execution and its focus on color nuances of the sun falling across the architecture and the foreground plaza. For Remington to make a work void of a figure or an animal was certainly atypical. It was on this trip, a difficult one for Remington due to his ballooned size, that his artistic frustration became fully realized. He wrote to his wife from Santa Fe on November 6, 1900, "This is election night and the town is very much excited. Reports are favorable to McK[inley] but can't tell yet. I am either going to do Pueblos or not and don't yet know. I think I won't. They don't

The Arizona Cowboy, *1901, pastel and graphite on paper. The Rockwell Museum, Corning, New York*

appeal to me — too decorative — and too easily in reach of every tenderfoot. Shall never come west again — It is all brick building — derby hats and blue overalls — it spoils my early illusions — and they are my capital. I have had a hard trip — eating all hours — all food — dirty and not much killing [?]." This often quoted letter is signed, "Frederic the Past."

Color became the focus for Remington. He read and re-read various publications on the uses of color and even brought all of his insights together about 1900 by annotating his copy of *Watercolor Painting: Description of Materials with Directions for Their use in Elementary Practice*, written by H.W. Herrick. He challenged himself to master a new medium, pastel, which can be seen in two works, *The Arizona Cowboy* (page 75) and the *Infantry Soldier* (page 77). The rapid progress the artist was able to make

Done in the Open, *1902, book, published by R. H. Russell. Mr. and Mrs. A. P. Hays*

was amazing. *The Arizona Cowboy* was one of eight pastels of various sizes created during 1901 for a portfolio of prints published by R.H. Russell, "A Bunch of Buckskins." Remington was pleased with his results, feeling the color so bright people would be stopped at a shop window when passing them by. The eight pastels along with a group of paintings were exhibited later in the year at the Clausen Gallery in New York, an exhibition Remington called his first as a real painter. The silhouette image of the mounted Arizona cowboy was truthful to the compositional technique Remington had established. It is the combination of color in the articulation of the horse and the briefly noted shadow below which demonstrated the artist's new thinking. His method remained fairly elementary and linear in this pastel, but when compared to the *Infantry Soldier* which appeared the following year on the cover of Russell's folio size book, *Done in the Open,* a change is noticeable. The blue blouse of the soldier is created in a less linear fashion with different blues being blended to create folds and shadows. The same is true of the trooper's pants which include multiple color blends. Compared with an earlier subject such as *Lt. Hardie* (1892) or *Lt. Johnson* (1889) where the artist pre-

Infantry Soldier, *1901, pastel on paper. Amon Carter Museum, Fort Worth, Texas*

blended a color and predominantly used it in the execution of the figure, these later works are more sophisticated.

Encouraged by the public success of "A Bunch of Buckskins" and *Done in the Open,* Remington quickly entered into a project with *Scribner's* to create a pictorial essay of four western "types," and allowed one of the paintings, *The Cowboy* (page 79), to be reproduced as a color print for sale through the magazine. Remington's new color abilities were evident. Drawing on his experience across the desert southwest, the artist represented the cowboy in wild action, staying atop his horse which is careening down a mountainside. The soft beauty of the location is opposite in feeling to the strident action of the painting. Careful attention to details such as the uplifted holster and the shadow of the cowboy's outstretched hand are trademark Remington, who truly understood the shifting weight of such action. It is the artist's new sensitivity to the landscape and mood which is beginning to develop. The desert ground is no longer harshly colored and severely contrasted. Rather, through blending color and trying to create an overall color harmony, the work takes on a beauty unlike earlier paintings.

By 1903 when the painter had signed a new contract with *Collier's* to provide a painting of his choice for monthly reproduction, his new method was fairly refined. One of Remington's greatest paintings, *Fight for the Waterhole* (page 81), best exemplifies the artist's direction during his final years. The image carries forth the artist's dramatic use of the "Last Stand" as representing the metaphor for the life and death struggle for migration and progress. As early as 1888 Remington established this motif and constantly returned to it throughout his career. In this case, the struggle has at least two interpretive layers, one being the plight of the five defenders against their adversaries, and the second, the realization of water as a precious commodity in the harsh desert lands of the Southwest. The subject itself can also be seen as nostalgic in two ways. One is the artist's return to the last stand concept. The other is the independent cowboy defending himself against the marauding Indian and the harsh environment, a rather heroic image. The viewer is given the innate sense that all five cowboys will ride out of their predicament due to the expression of confidence on the face of the foreground figure, and the overall sense of beauty to the landscape. Similar to the technique of *The Cowboy,* the subtle blending of colors and overall harmony adopted by the painter, seem to override the anxiety of the moment. Remington's conscious effort to extend his reality of the late 19th century West into the present century was a personal struggle which resulted in critical ambivalence.

Remington's persona was so entrenched in his role as illustrator that it has been difficult for art historians and critics to see him any other way. His self-promotion, driven by his desire for success was likewise a barrier. In addition, museums and American art collectors shied away from acquiring his paintings for decades.

The multiple interpretations of Remington's work since his death proves his importance to America's art. His position is being re-examined again as a result of the revisionist historical methodology of the past decade. As this dialogue continues into the next decade, Remington's

The Cowboy, *1902, oil on canvas. Amon Carter Museum, Fort Worth, Texas*

Waterhole, Sierra Bonitas, Arizona, *before 1890, photograph by Frederic Remington. Frederic Remington Art Museum, Ogdensburg, New York*

career will take on greater significance. This is a tribute to the artist's rich complexity, but it also results in occasional overinterpretations. A 1991 exhibition of western American art, "The West as America," held at the National Museum of American Art has been the most visible and successful effort in this arena. Alex Nemerov, in the catalogue, explored in depth Remington's *Fight for the Waterhole* as part of an essay on the nostalgia of the West. He viewed Remington's late career as being nostalgic, one of three mediations which in general reveal obsessions in western American paintings. The other two were art by other artists and the act of painting itself. The point made was that each of these characteristics was an unavoidable obstacle to a realistic retrieval of the past. Remington hinted throughout his career that he was not trying to be purely authentic. He did rely on his reportorial reactions to situations which created the ambivalence of his personality, particularly pertaining to the Buffalo Soldiers and the Mexican cavalry, and he confused this issue by his willingness to be promoted as representing actual events in his art. He was also prone to succumbing to his own publicity.

The artist utilized realistic detail to create an immediacy between the painting and the viewer. As Nemerov pointed out in *Fight for the Waterhole,* the guns are delineated to be exact, this being a segue used by many artists to bring the viewer into a believable scene. Remington also placed

Sketch for "Fight for the Waterhole," *c. 1903, oil on board. Buffalo Bill Historical Center, Cody, Wyoming, Gift of the Coe Foundation*

Fight for the Waterhole, *1903, oil on canvas. Museum of Fine Arts, Houston, Texas, The Hogg Brothers Collection, Gift of Miss Ima Hogg*

the activity of this drama in a real setting by utilizing a small photograph he had taken in Arizona years earlier (page 80). The artist's dependence on a photograph in this case is a nostalgic act of reminiscence, but it also is a convenience to place his "Last Stand" in an authentic environment. The development of this painting is atypical for the artist because an interim oil sketch of the Sierra Bonitas waterhole was also made (page 80), creating the characteristics of light the painter desired. All of this effort signals that *Fight for the Waterhole* was intended to be a major picture.

Later writers, prone to current interpretations of history, struggle to put an artist into a contemporary context. Quite often this process creates conflict. There is a tendency to sometimes ignore the artist's intentions and define the work of art within the critic's or the historian's own beliefs. To view a painting in this manner is not incorrect on a personal level, but the ideal of the historian, to objectively view history with all resources available, is ignored. As Arthur Schlesinger pointed out in his recent book, *The Disuniting of America,* "Historians must always strive toward the unattainable ideal of objectivity. But as we respond to contemporary urgencies, we sometimes exploit the past for nonhistorical purposes, taking from the past, or projecting upon it, what suits our own society or ideology." Nemerov's interpretation of *Fight for the Waterhole* serves as model for this process. He first adopts Richard Slotkin's revisionist theory that the last stand, so prevalent in late 19th century western American art, was "a powerful metaphor in the industrialized eastern United States." Taken further, such scenes are seen by Slotkin and Nemerov as an allegory to the plight of capitalization in an era of frequent conflict between labor and management. This is not a debate into which Remington entered. As the writer focuses on the picture, one learns the shells laying on the ground are the equivalent of the supine cowboys, and the randomness of the spent shells represent there being no outside controlling hand. The used cartridges, shadows, and diminishing water represents the passage of time, as does the location of each cowboy on this clock-like shape of the sink itself. Granted, the shadow is an artist's mechanism to give a time of day, but it must be remembered it is a way to define real space. To equivocate shadow covering the legs of one figure to burial, as Nemerov does, is difficult to understand because his legs are lost to the undulating geography, not shade. The writer then sums up the significance of this great painting, "The over determination of *Fight for the Waterhole* with its disconsonant mix of powerful realism and an equally powerful metahistorical counter-realism, expresses the intellectual complexity of Remington's historical vision." Nemerov's goal is a good one, to try to take Remington out of his cast as creating a "permanent record" and put him into a more interpretive role. This should be the ideal of the historian. However, when this act is made it should be done in a manner that clearly admits the contemporary context of the discussion. Remington would never have imagined such an interpretation of his great painting; however, he would be complimented that it took on a timeless quality which allowed it to teach people of future generations of their own attitudes and aspirations.

One of the major reasons *Collier's* in 1903 was willing to place Remington under such a lucrative contract, one thousand dollars per month for a picture's reproduction rights, was the return they expected on their investment. As the artist's name became affiliated with the monthly magazine, circulation did increase. The magazine also advertised colored prints of the paintings to be available for one dollar fifty cents through the mail. Knowing the renown this could bring to him, the artist at first attacked his work for *Collier's* with a new seriousness which is borne out by the first few works reproduced. *Fight for the Waterhole* began from a small photograph from which an oil sketch was executed and then a finished work was made into color prints. This cycle demonstrates a sincere desire by the artist.

Remington, unfortunately, began thinking of his arrangement with *Collier's* as simply a financial one. The artistic challenge faded quickly, to the extent the artist conceived a series each year and tried quickly to complete these works so he could pursue other projects. The pictures submitted to *Collier's* late in 1904 comprised a series relating to the Louisiana Purchase being commemorated that year, and included images such as

"Great Explorers Series, The Expedition of Coronado," *1905–1906, color prints, published by Collier's. Thomas Gilcrease Institute of American History and Art, Tulsa, Oklahoma*

"The Pioneers," "The Santa Fe Trade," and "End of the Day." The following year the artist continued this theme and produced a series of "Great Explorers" (page 83) depicting Hernando de Soto, Francisco Coronado, Radisson and Grosseiliers, and others. These works, historical illustrations, far from Remington's experiences, failed as paintings even though thousands of prints sold. His final series, "Tragedy of the Trees," was so poorly received in 1906 (six of twelve being published) that Remington, recognized his mistake of the past three years, and on February 8, 1907, burned all of the canvases save one, *Radisson and Grosseiliers.* These three series signify an artist who made the wrong decision trying to become a historical subject painter struggling for material. He needed firsthand experience with his subject, a fact well proven over the prior two decades of his career. Remington stated in his diary following his bonfire outside his studio, the only works remaining were his landscape sketches. Since moving his summer studio to an island on the St. Lawrence River near Ogdensburg several years earlier he had been at work on landscape studies and the study of moonlight. This interest most likely explains the success of the *Radisson and Grosseiliers* painting because it represented the two French explorers who came down "Remington's river," three and a half centuries earlier. He was able to place the Frenchmen and their native American co-travelers in an environment he fully comprehended.

Putting his mistakes behind him, and to a degree humbling himself by losing his *Collier's* contract, 1907 can be seen as a year of decision for Remington. Having gained confidence as a landscape painter during the previous four years by making studies in upstate New York, he realized he could no longer be an illustrator. An activity during 1907 which helped the situation was the work on a $20,000 commission from Philadelphia's Fairmont Park Association for a monumental bronze cowboy which was installed early the next year. Remington again dipped into his southwestern experiences to bring forth a new direction in his work. The artist was also encouraged by the sale of half of his ten-painting exhibition held at the prestigious Knoedler Gallery during December of 1906. *Against the Sunset* (private collection) dominated the exhibition with its vivid orange sunset against which a silhouetted cowboy literally flew on a speeding horse. There was no detail in the work. Remington had finally blended the nostalgia of his experience in the Southwest with the color he had been striving to perfect since the turn of the century. What were to be the last three years of the artist's life would also be his most praised as a fine painter.

The following year thirteen paintings were hung in a Knoedler exhibition, including *Last Lull in the Fight* placed in the window. One of the most notable new paintings was *Fired On* (page 85), a nocturnal scene depicting a small cavalry troop arrested by gunfire at water's edge from an unseen adversary. The subject, derived from earlier experiences with the cavalry in the Southwest, followed the formula of *Against the Sunset.* Detail is shrouded by the night so that the subject becomes the terror of attack and is communicated by the lead horse and rider. Recent scholarship by Nemerov acknowledges the painter's ability to successfully create the foreground space by powerfully modeling the white horse with a rich, thickly painted "swirl of paint" and a rich "slather of impasto." The writer carries the metaphor of the paint surface too far, however, by suggesting the horse is terrified "of the splashes of water that formally echo its own tail." He concludes, trying to convince the reader that such a paint surface denies reality, by stating the horse's fear and artist's, too, arise from realizing the horse's body "is nothing more than paint and canvas." Conversely, the actual fear in a scene like this was more likely to have been a sharp gunshot ringing out in the night which would startle animal and trooper alike. The splashes of water and the wide-eyed looks are the visual equivalents of the sound, a technique the artist had used for twenty years. *Fired On* was to be a very significant work for Remington because two years after its exhibition, William Evans, the great collector of Tonalist paintings, acquired the work for his collection which was then donated to what is today the National Museum of American Art. It was the first painting acquired from the artist for a museum, symbolic of Remington's acceptance with his colleagues such as Willard Metcalf and Childe Hassam.

Fired On, *1907, oil on canvas. National Museum of American Art, Smithsonian Institution, Gift of William T. Evans*

A second painting shown in that year's exhibition was the most ambitious as to size and complexity of figures. It was titled in the catalogue, *On the Southern Plains* (page 87), and in many ways was a summation painting for Remington. He brought forward the action which had made him famous in such works as *A Dash for the Timber,* or *Captain Dodge's Colored Troopers to the Rescue,* yet he updated the scene slightly from his observation of Metcalf and Hassam, the Impressionists for whom he had the greatest respect, by adopting a color mix and jagged brush stroke, best seen in the shadows of the horses. The movement of the brush stroke lies on an angle from lower right to upper left and is crossed by the implied action of the charging horses. The intersection of these two types of movement accentuates the action. The painter quietly painted the troopers' bedrolls a pastel green to harmonize the painting. Nostalgic because this work represents plains military action from the 1860s, the beauty of the action itself diverts the pure historicism of the subject. Unable to rely solely on the color and action of the moment, Remington chose to symbolize his nostalgia, just as he had years earlier in *Wounded Bunkie* by includ-

Eight New Remington Paintings, *1909, color print portfolio, published by Collier's. Arizona West Galleries, Scottsdale, Arizona*

ing a bleached buffalo skull in the center foreground. Though unsold in the exhibition, *On the Southern Plains* was included in a color print portfolio for sale two years later by *Collier's* (page 86). The final compliment to this painting and to the artist was its acquisition by fifteen gentlemen, two years after the artist's 1909 death, for the Metropolitan Museum of Art.

Not all of the artist's late pictures were action oriented (page 90). Recalling the desert ranches he visited twenty years earlier which appeared "to be little more than a cattle station," Remington created quiet moody scenes such as *Waiting in the Moonlight* (page 88). A woman wrapped with a dark shawl over her white skirt waits in the street of a crude frontier town, where a cowboy stops to speak with her. Since she keeps her back turned to him, he must not be the reason she waits. For several years the nocturne had played an important role in Remington's development as a painter. Inspired originally by the California painter, Charles Rollo Peters, Remington sought to perfect the palette of moonlight through careful observation, especially during his summers away from the city. Generally, he utilized a bluish or greenish overall tone to capture night light, but it was important to have strong contrasts which reflected the soft moonlight. The main figure in *Waiting in the Moonlight* presents the lightest and darkest tones, so that the rest of the picture is developed secondarily to the main subject. This kind of intimate moment was typical of genteel painters at the turn of the century, and Remington has merely

On the Southern Plains, *1907–1908, oil on canvas. Metropolitan Museum of Art, New York, New York, Gift of Several Gentlemen, 1911*

transported the scene to the frontier towns he remembered in the southwest United States during his visits beginning as early as 1885.

The final remembrance of Remington's Southwest can be seen metaphorically in his portrait of Major General Leonard Wood (page 89) begun during September, 1909, three months prior to the artist's unexpected death. Exhibited in the Knoedler show of that year, Remington strove to commemorate the military success of Wood who was the base surgeon at Fort Huachuca in southern Arizona when Remington first visited during the 1880s. Wood joined with Lawton in the capture of Geronimo. As with other military figures, Remington stayed in communication because of the help his friend could offer. Wood was a co-leader of the "Rough Riders" with Theodore Roosevelt during the Spanish American War of 1898 and in command of the Division of the Philippines during "Roosevelt's" war. According to Wood's diary, Remington and the General were in attendance at a dinner honoring Buffalo Bill Cody in New York City on May 12, 1909, when Remington was "anxious that I should come up and spend a day with him and go over the Geronimo business with him." Finally on September 4, Wood sent his horses out to Remington's new estate at Ridgefield, Connecticut, with one of his officers, and himself boarded a train. Upon arrival they spoke late into the evening about Arizona and old times.

Waiting in the Moonlight, *c. 1907, oil on canvas. Frederic Remington Art Museum, Ogdensburg, New York*

The next day Wood recalled in his journal, they got down to work, "He [Remington] selected the bay, Walking John, as the horse to be used, and I turned out in regular khaki, campaign hat, saber, etc. Whitman Saddle, and he worked for about 2½ hours in the morning and resumed work again after lunch. He got in the bulk of his framework for the sketch and filled in sufficiently to give him an idea of the color value under the conditions of light." The next day, prior to Wood's departure the artist took "some Kodaks as a check on details of equipment, etc which [had] changed since his last days on the Frontier." Wood was unable to see the

Portrait of Major General Leonard Wood, *1909, oil on canvas. The West Point Museum, United States Military Academy, West Point, New York*

portrait until he visited Knoedler's for the exhibition, even though Remington encouraged him to come to the studio. He felt "Remington's picture good in many respects, pose good, horse good, seat on horse good, but face rather tough." Wood's reaction could have been made twenty years earlier because the artist always struggled in the handling of a human face, but he had the horses and other details well in command. In many ways Remington's art had stayed the same through his tumultuous years of challenge and change.

What was to be Frederic Remington's final exhibition opened at Knoedler Gallery on November 29, where it hung for two weeks. Twenty-two works in addition to the Wood portrait were hung, including six small landscape paintings. All of the other works were inspired by northern plains experiences. His exhibition, for the first time, met with critical acclaim in New York. His December 9 diary entry read, "The art critics have all come down — I have belated but splendid notices from all the papers. They ungrudgingly give me a high place as a 'mere painter' I have been on their trail a long while and they never surrendered while they had a leg to stand on. The 'Illustrator' phase has become background. But my sales are disappointing why I don't know." Remington obviously wanted the gold ring because Knoedler records show that eleven of the twenty-three works in the exhibition were sold. The painter was not able to relish in conquering the critics because fifteen days following the close of his exhibition, Remington died unexpectedly from complications following an emergency appendectomy.

Apaches Listening, *c. 1908, oil on canvas. Frederic Remington Art Museum, Ogdensburg, New York*

Had Remington lived it has often been conjectured that his popularity as a painter would have continued to rise. Even if that had been true, the importance of the Southwest in his art would most likely have dwindled. As he had turned more toward landscape imagery during his later years, he was drawn to the wide open Great Plains states, upstate New York and Connecticut because these regions offered the subtle tonal changes he was attempting to capture on his canvases. The Southwest would no longer have offered the inspiration it had through the previous twenty-five years. Each time the artist sought to shift his approach or confront a new challenge, he had drawn on the rich experiences he recalled as a young maturing artist traveling in "his Southwest." It was there he developed his reputation of being America's military artist. It was there he discovered the heroic figure of the cowboy and the vaquero. Through these individuals Remington created an action-packed interpretation of the West which lived through four generations, and is only now being challenged for not being as inclusive as it could have been, given the diversity of the developing West. That Remington's art continues to intrigue the viewer and confront the scholar is testimony to his importance. That the Southwest and its inhabitants is at the forefront of this dialogue proves how critical the region was to this great American artist's development.

Exhibition Checklist — *Frederic Remington's Southwest*

All dimensions listed are in inches, height precedes width.

Agency Near Sill (In the Betting Ring — Comanches), 1889, oil on canvas (black and white), 25 × 35
Collection IBM Corporation, Armonk, New York
(page 3)

The Apaches Are Coming, 1885, pen and ink, wash and gouache on paper, 12¼ × 17½
Frederic Remington Art Museum, Ogdensburg, New York *(page 11)*

Apaches Listening, c. 1908, oil on canvas, 20 × 26
Frederic Remington Art Museum, Ogdensburg, New York *(page 90)*

The Arizona Cowboy, 1901, pastel and graphite on paper, 30 × 24
The Rockwell Museum, Corning, New York
(page 75) *(Phoenix only)*

Arizona Territory 1888 (or Marching in the Desert), 1888, oil on canvas (black and white), 18 × 28
University of Wyoming, American Heritage Center, Gift of the Rentschler and Rita Cushman Families *(page 22)*

Army Mule with Harness Marks, n.d., oil on canvas, 19⅛ × 24¼
Buffalo Bill Historical Center, Cody, Wyoming, Gift of the Coe Foundation *(page 73)*

Attack on the Supply Train, 1885, watercolor on paper, 13½ × 28⅞
James R. Williams Trust *(page 15)*

Bread Man, Mexico, c. 1893, pencil on blue toned paper, 11½ × 8¾
Frederic Remington Art Museum, Ogdensburg, New York *(page 43)*

Bronco Buster, 1895, bronze (Roman Bronze Works cast no. 7), 23¼ × 22⅜ × 11⅝
Maricopa County Historical Society, Desert Caballeros Western Museum, Wickenburg, Arizona *(page 68)*

Bullfight in Mexico, 1889, oil on canvas, 24 × 32
Santa Barbara Museum of Art, California, Gift of Mrs. Sterling Morton to the Sterling Morton Collection *(page 42)*

Cavalry in an Arizona Sandstorm, 1889, oil on canvas (black and white), 22⅛ × 35¼
Amon Carter Museum, Fort Worth, Texas *(page 33)*

Cavalryman's Breakfast on the Plains, c. 1892, oil on canvas, 22⅛ × 32⅛
Amon Carter Museum, Fort Worth, Texas *(page 55)*

Cavalryman of the Line, Mexico, 1889, oil on canvas, 24⅛ × 20
Amon Carter Museum, Fort Worth, Texas *(page 45)*

Chicken Man, Mexico, c. 1893, pencil on blue toned paper, 12 × 9
Frederic Remington Art Museum, Ogdensburg, New York *(page 43)*

Powhatan H. Clarke, 1889–1890, oil on canvas, 10¼ × 13
Frederic Remington Art Museum, Ogdensburg, New York *(page 26)*

Comanche Brave, Fort Reno, 1888, oil on canvas, 24½ × 20
Collection of W. B. Ruger *(page 4)*

The Cowboy, 1902, oil on canvas, 40¼ × 27⅛
Amon Carter Museum, Fort Worth, Texas *(page 79)*

The Cowboy, c. 1889, oil on board, 27¼ × 17½ (sight)
The Rockwell Museum, Corning, New York, Gift of Mrs. Hilary Barratt-Brown *(Memphis and Omaha only)*

Cowboys on a Cattle Thief's Trail, 1885, watercolor on paper, 11¼ × 17
The Bill and Irma Runyon Art Collections, MSC Forsyth Center Galleries, Texas A & M University, College Station *(page 13)* *(Phoenix only)*

Captain Dodge's Colored Troopers to the Rescue, 1891, tempera on paper, 18⅝ × 35⅞
Mrs. Charles Steward Mott Collection, Courtesy of the Flint Institute of Arts, Michigan *(page 59)*

Drum Corps, Mexican Army, 1889, oil on panel, 18 × 28
Amon Carter Museum, Fort Worth, Texas *(page 38)*

Fight for the Waterhole, 1903, oil on canvas, 27 × 40
Museum of Fine Arts, Houston, Texas, The Hogg Brothers Collection, Gift of Miss Ima Hogg
(page 81) *(Phoenix only)*

Sketch for "Fight for the Waterhole," c. 1903, oil on board, 12 × 17⅞
Buffalo Bill Historical Center, Cody, Wyoming, Gift of the Coe Foundation *(page 80)*

Fired On, 1907, oil on canvas, 27⅛ × 40
National Museum of American Art, Smithsonian Institution, Gift of William T. Evans *(page 85)*

The Gendarme, City of Mexico, 1889, watercolor on paper, 17 × 12⅞
Museum of Fine Arts, Houston, Texas, The Hogg Brothers Collection, Gift of Miss Ima Hogg
(page 40)

Geronimo and His Band Returning From a Raid Into Mexico, c. 1888, oil on canvas (black and white), 28×21
From the Collection of Mr. and Mrs. M. Pfeffer
(page 25)

The Half-wild Cattle Come Down From the Hills, 1896, pen and ink wash on paper, $20\frac{7}{8} \times 25\frac{3}{8}$
Phoenix Art Museum, Arizona, Carl S. Dentzel Collection *(page 47)*

Lt. Hardie, c. 1892, watercolor on paper, 17×10
Frederic Remington Art Museum, Ogdensburg, New York *(page 62)*

Holding Up the Pay Escort (or The Hold-up), c. 1894, watercolor on paper, 20×28
Valley National Bank of Arizona, Phoenix
(page 64)

An Incident on the March, 1891, pen and ink and wash on cardboard, $16\frac{9}{16} \times 21\frac{7}{8}$
The Carnegie Museum of Art, Pittsburgh, Pennsylvania, Andrew Carnegie Fund *(page 57)*

The Infantryman, 1890, watercolor on paper, 18×10
Harriet Russell Stanley Fund 52.16, New Britain Museum of American Art, Connecticut *(page 58)*

Infantry Soldier, 1901, pastel on paper, $29 \times 15\frac{7}{8}$
Amon Carter Museum, Fort Worth, Texas
(page 77) *(Phoenix only)*

Interrogating Mexican Bandits (or The Three Bandits Were Led Back into the Path), 1899, pen and ink wash on paper, 27×40
Mr. and Mrs. William Healey *(page 53)*

Lt. Carter Johnson, c. 1889, watercolor on paper, $17\frac{1}{2} \times 11\frac{1}{2}$
Mr. and Mrs. Jerry S. Handler *(page 31)*

Lt. Carter Johnson, c. 1889, watercolor on paper, $13\frac{1}{2} \times 8\frac{1}{2}$
Private Collection, Courtesy Graham Gallery, New York *(page 30)*

Leaving the Canyon, c. 1889, pen and ink wash on paper, $24\frac{3}{4} \times 19\frac{3}{4}$ (sight)
Gene Autry Western Heritage Museum, Los Angeles, California *(page 28)*

Mexican Cavalry on the Move (or Revolution in Northern Mexico — Marching Regulars to the Front), 1893, oil on canvas, $22\frac{7}{8} \times 34\frac{13}{16}$
U.S. Cavalry Museum, Department of the Army, Fort Riley, Kansas *(page 50)*

Mexican Doorways, 1891, pen and ink wash on paper, 18×27
The University of Arizona Museum of Art, Tucson, Gift of Mr. and Mrs. Harry L. Bell *(page 41)*

Mexican Engineer, 1889, oil on canvas, $28\frac{1}{2} \times 19$
Frederic Remington Art Museum, Ogdensburg, New York *(page 39)*

Mexican Major, c. 1889, oil on canvas, $34\frac{1}{4} \times 49\frac{1}{8}$
The Art Institute of Chicago, George F. Harding Collection *(page 36)*

The Mexican Vaquero, 1890, oil on canvas, $32\frac{1}{2} \times 23$
The Art Institute of Chicago, George F. Harding Collection *(page 44)*

Mexican Vaqueros Breaking a Bronc, 1897, pen and ink and wash drawing, $26\frac{1}{4} \times 38\frac{1}{2}$
Museum of Fine Arts, Boston, Massachusetts, Bequest of John T. Spaulding, 48.874 *(page 52)*

Modern Comanche, 1890, oil on canvas, 33×23
The Bill and Irma Runyon Art Collections, MSC Forsyth Center Galleries, Texas A & M University, College Station *(page 34)* *(Phoenix Only)*

On the Southern Plains, 1907–1908, oil on canvas, $30\frac{1}{8} \times 51\frac{1}{8}$
Metropolitan Museum of Art, New York, New York, Gift of Several Gentlemen, 1911 *(page 87)*

The Outlaw, 1906, bronze (Roman Bronze Works cast no. 4), $22\frac{3}{4} \times 13\frac{3}{4} \times 8\frac{1}{4}$
Private Collection, Paradise Valley, Arizona *(page 70)*

Padron, Mexico, c. 1893, pencil on gray paper, 12×9
Frederic Remington Art Museum, Ogdensburg, New York *(page 43)*

A Pitching Bronc, 1892, ink wash on paper, $17 \times 13\frac{1}{2}$
Mrs. William A. Seifert, Jr. *(page 61)*

The Rattlesnake, 1905, bronze (Roman Bronze Works cast no. 48), $20\frac{1}{4} \times 16 \times 14$
Mr. William H. Brophy II *(page 69)*

Roasting the Christmas Beef in a Cavalry Camp, c. 1892, oil on canvas, $29\frac{1}{8} \times 45\frac{1}{16}$
Yale University Art Gallery, New Haven, Connecticut, Gift of Mrs. Dorothy Knox Goodyear Rogers in Memory of Edmund Pendleton Rogers *(page 56)*

Captain Albert Seiber, n.d., pen and ink on paper, 9×12
Frederic Remington Art Museum, Ogdensburg, New York *(page 20)*

Signalling the Main Command, 1885, watercolor on paper, 22×32
James R. Williams Trust *(page 19)*

Skirmish Line — Target Practice, 1889, pencil, watercolor and gouache on paper, $18\frac{1}{2} \times 25\frac{1}{2}$
Private Collection, Courtesy Gerald Peters Gallery, Santa Fe, New Mexico *(page 27)*

Soledad, Mexico, 1896, pencil on paper, 9 × 11¼
Frederic Remington Art Museum, Ogdensburg, New York (*page 46*)

Soledad, Mexico, 1896, pencil on paper, 9 × 11¼
Frederic Remington Art Museum, Ogdensburg, New York (*page 46*)

Standing Figure (Texas), c. 1893, pencil on paper, 14¾ × 10¼
Frederic Remington Art Museum, Ogdensburg, New York (*page 6*)

Sunday Morning Toilet on the Ranch, 1885, watercolor on paper, 13½ × 17½
Collection of Charles R. Wood (*page 10*)

Texas, c. 1893, pencil and ink on gray paper, 7 × 9⅞
Frederic Remington Art Museum, Ogdensburg, New York (*page 16*)

Texas Cowboy, c. 1893, pencil on paper, 7 × 9¾
Frederic Remington Art Museum, Ogdensburg, New York (*page 17*)

They Left Him Thar in the Trail, c. 1895, pen and ink wash on paper, 29 × 21
Phoenix Art Museum, Arizona, Gift of Friends and Family in Memory of John W. Kieckhefer (*page 63*)

A Tumble from the Trail, c. 1888, oil on board (black and white), 28 × 18
Collection of Donald J. Sutherland, New York, New York (*page 23*)

Untitled (adobe pueblo with baking oven), c. 1900, oil on board, 12¼ × 18½
Buffalo Bill Historical Center, Cody, Wyoming, Gift of the Coe Foundation (*page 74*)

Vaquero, Soledad Ranch, Mexico, c. 1896, oil on canvas, 29¾ × 17¾
Maricopa County Historical Society, Desert Caballeros Western Museum, Wickenburg, Arizona (*page 48*)

Waiting in the Moonlight, c. 1907, oil on canvas, 27 × 30
Frederic Remington Art Museum, Ogdensburg, New York (*page 88*)

Water, 1892, pen and ink wash and gouache on paper, 17½ × 30¼
Frederic Remington Art Museum, Ogdensburg, New York (*page 60*)

Portrait of Major General Leonard Wood, 1909, oil on canvas, 40 × 40
The West Point Museum, United States Military Academy, West Point, New York (*page 89*)
(Memphis and Omaha only)

Wounded Bunkie, c. 1896, bronze (Henry-Bonnard Co. Founders, unnumbered cast), 20 × 22 × 12¼
Thomas Gilcrease Institute of American History and Art, Tulsa, Oklahoma (*page 71*)

JOURNALS

"Journal of a Trip Across the Continent through Arizona and Sonora Old Mexico," 1886, pencil on paper, 8½ × 5½
Robert Taft Collection, Kansas State Historical Society, Topeka (*page 14*)

Arizona, 1888, pencil on paper, 8½ × 5½
Robert Taft Collection, Kansas State Historical Society, Topeka (*page 21*)

Trip to Mexico, 1891 (?), pencil on paper, 9¾ × 4¾
Frederic Remington Art Museum, Ogdensburg, New York

Trip to Mexico, 1893 (?), pencil on paper, 9¾ × 4¾
Frederic Remington Art Museum, Ogdensburg, New York

LETTERS

From Remington to Powhatan H. Clarke
December 27, 1888
September 1, 1890
September 13, 1890
September 30, 1890

Missouri Historical Society, Powhatan H. Clarke Papers, Frederic Remington Letters (*pages 29, 32*)

From Remington to Owen Wister
January, 1895
c. 1894, Auditorium Hotel Stationery

Manuscript Division, Library of Congress, Washington, D.C. (*pages 51, 66*)

PHOTOGRAPHS

Putnam and Valentine, Los Angeles, California, *Arizona Indians,* 2$\frac{15}{16}$ × 3⅝
Frederic Remington Art Museum, Ogdensburg, New York (*page 12*)

Photographer unknown, *Officers of the 10th Cavalry, Ft. Grant, Arizona, c. 1890,* 5¼ × 8½
Frederic Remington Art Museum, Ogdensburg, New York (*page 29*)

Attributed to Frederic Remington, *Troops in Mexico City, 1891 or 1893,* 5¼ × 4¼
Frederic Remington Art Museum, Ogdensburg, New York (*page 37*)

Attributed to Frederic Remington, *Vaquero, Mexico, 1891 or 1893,* 5¼ × 4¼
Frederic Remington Art Museum, Ogdensburg, New York *(page 49)*

Frederic Remington, *Waterhole, Sierra Bonitas, Arizona, before 1890,* 1¼ × 2¾
Frederic Remington Art Museum, Ogdensburg, New York *(page 80)*

PRINTS AND BOOKS

Cow-boys of Arizona — Roused by a Scout, wood engraving (redrawn by W.A. Rogers), *Harper's Weekly,* February 25, 1882, Arizona State Department of Library, Archives, and Public Records, Research Division, Phoenix *(page 5)*

The Rescue of Corporal Scott, wood engraving, *Harper's Weekly,* August 21, 1886, Arizona State Department of Library, Archives, and Public Records, Research Division, Phoenix *(page 18)*

Cavalry in an Arizona Sandstorm, wood engraving, *Harper's Weekly,* September 14, 1889, Arizona State Department of Library, Archives, and Public Records, Research Division, Phoenix

Roasting the Christmas Beef, wood engraving, *Harper's Weekly,* December 24, 1892, Arizona State Department of Library, Archives, and Public Records, Research Division, Phoenix *(page 56)*

Done in the Open, 1902, book, published by R.H. Russell
Mr. and Mrs. A.P. Hays *(page 76)*

Eight New Remington Paintings, 1909, color print portfolio, published by Colliers, 11½ × 16½
Arizona West Galleries, Scottsdale, Arizona *(page 86)*

Frederic Remington, *Fight for the Waterhole, 1903,* color print, published by Collier's, 10¾ × 15½
Thomas Gilcrease Institute of American History and Art, Tulsa, Oklahoma

Frederic Remington, *"Great Explorers Series," 1905–1906,* color prints, published by Collier's, various sizes
Thomas Gilcrease Institute of American History and Art, Tulsa, Oklahoma *(page 83)*

Selected Bibliography

Ballinger, James K., *Frederic Remington,* New York, 1989.

Frederic Remington Art Museum, Ogdensburg, New York, Frederic Remington Archives.

Harper, Henry J., *The House of Harper,* New York, 1912.

Hassrick, Peter H., *Frederic Remington: Paintings, Drawings and Sculpture in the Amon Carter Museum and Sid W. Richardson Foundation Collections,* New York, 1973.

Kansas State Historical Society, Topeka, The Robert Taft Papers.

Library of Congress, Manuscript Division, Washington, D.C., Owen Wister and Leonard Wood Papers.

McCracken, Harold, *Frederic Remington: Artist of the Old West,* Philadelphia, 1947.

McCracken, Harold, *The Frederic Remington Book: A Pictorial History of the West,* Garden City, New York, 1966.

Missouri Historical Society, Saint Louis, Powhatan H. Clarke Papers.

Nemerov, Alex, "Frederic Remington: Within and Without the Past," *American Art,* Oxford University Press in association with the National Museum of American Art, Smithsonian Institution, Winter/Spring 1991, Vol. 5, Numbers 1–2.

Samuels, Peggy and Samuels, Harold, *Frederic Remington: A Biography,* New York, 1982.

Samuels, Peggy and Samuels, Harold, *Remington: The Complete Prints,* New York, 1990.

Samuels, Peggy and Samuels, Harold, eds., *The Collected Writings of Frederic Remington,* Garden City, New York, 1979.

Shapiro, Michael Edward, and Hassrick, Peter H., with essays by David G. McCullough, Doreen Bolger Burke, and John Seelye, *Frederic Remington: The Masterworks,* exhibition catalogue, Saint Louis, Missouri, 1988.

Splete, Allen P. and Splete, Marilyn D., *Frederic Remington — Selected Letters,* New York, 1988.

Truettner, William H., ed., with contributions by Nancy K. Anderson . . . [et al.], *The West as America: Reinterpreting Images of the Frontier, 1820–1920,* exhibition catalogue, National Museum of American Art, Washington, D.C., 1991.

The United States Military Academy, *Frederic Remington: The Soldier Artist,* exhibition catalogue, The West Point Museum, New York, 1979.

Vorpahl, Ben Merchant, ed., *My Dear Wister: The Frederic Remington-Owen Wister Letters,* Palo Alto, California, 1972.

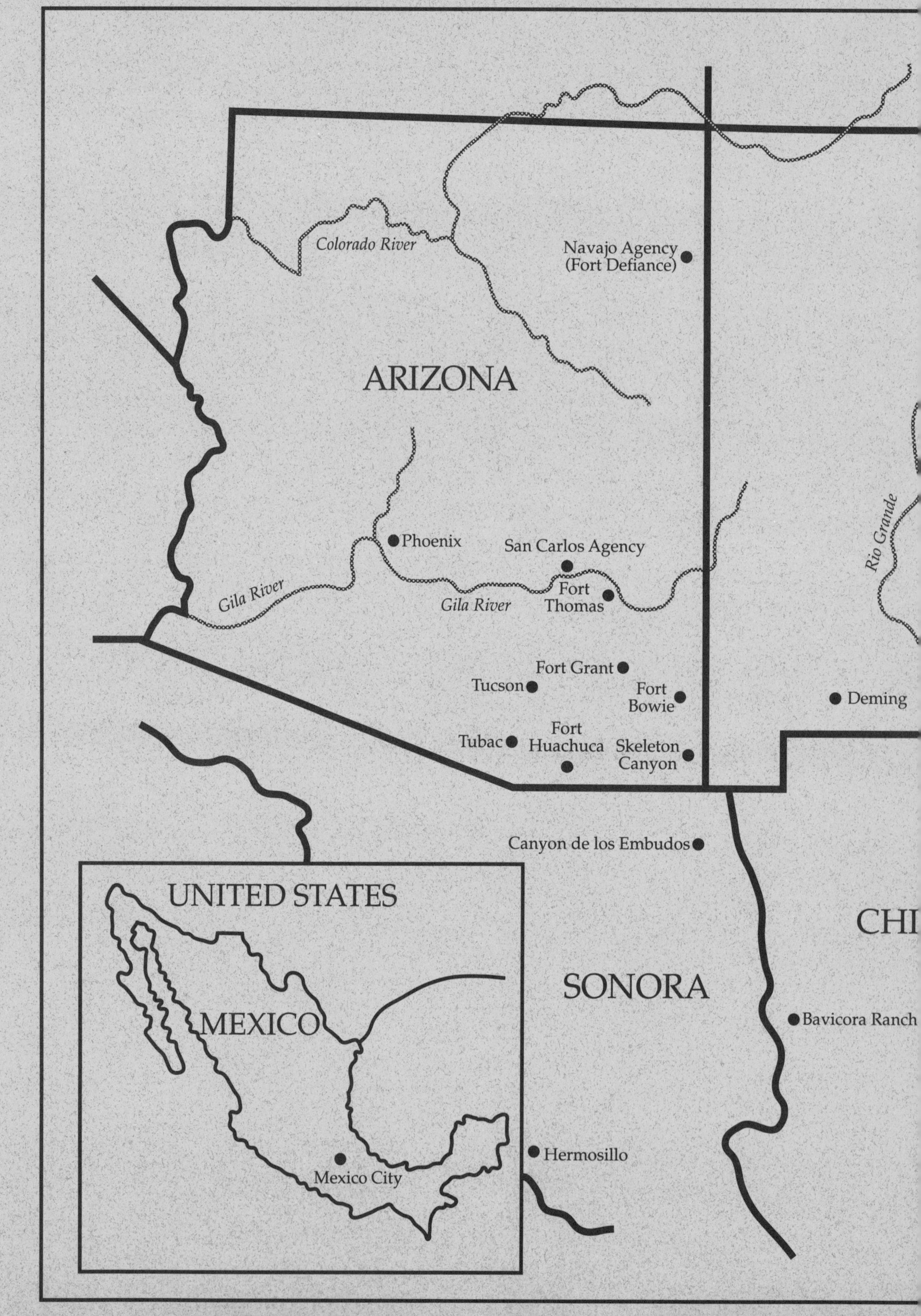

Colorado River
Navajo Agency
(Fort Defiance)
ARIZONA
Phoenix
San Carlos Agency
Gila River
Gila River
Fort
Thomas
Rio Grande
Fort Grant
Tucson
Fort
Bowie
Deming
Tubac
Fort
Huachuca
Skeleton
Canyon
Canyon de los Embudos
UNITED STATES
MEXICO
Mexico City
CHI
SONORA
Bavicora Ranch
Hermosillo